A Magical Guide to
Finding the Love of
Your Life

Enchantments
of the Heart

By
Dorothy Morrison

NEW PAGE BOOKS
A division of The Career Press, Inc.
Franklin Lakes, NJ

Copyright © 2002 by Dorothy Morrison

Enchantments of the Heart
Edited by Jodi Brandon
Typeset by Eileen Dow Munson
Cover design by Cheryl Cohan Finbow
Printed in the U.S.A. by Book-mart Press

To order this title, please call toll-free 1-800-CAREER-1 (NJ and Canada: 201-848-0310) to order using VISA or MasterCard, or for further information on books from Career Press.

The Career Press, Inc., 3 Tice Road, PO Box 687,
Franklin Lakes, NJ 07417
www.careerpress.com
www.newpagebooks.com

Library of Congress Cataloging-in-Publication Data

Morrison, Dorothy, 1955-
    Enchantments of the heart : a magical guide to finding the love of your life / by Dorothy Morrison.
       p. cm.
    Includes bibliographical references and index.
    ISBN 1-56414-546-8 (pbk.)
    1. Magic. 2. Love—Miscellanea. I. Title.

BF1623.L6 M675 2002
133.4'42—dc21

                                 20011044267

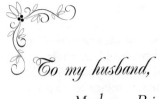

To my husband,

Mark, my Prince and the love of my life,
who continually reminds me that
true love and romance are not only the
ultimate magics,
but that they're alive and well and
dancing in our hearts...

and to his mother,

Ann,
who brought him into this world
and raised him to be the
Prince of my dreams.

Acknowledgments

Writing this book was much like living a fairy tale. There were magical moments of wonder and awe, days when the sun smiled upon me without fail, and nights when the moon enchanted all in Her view. My very existence seemed charmed. No matter where I stepped or how far I wandered, things just fell into place. Life was good, magic was afoot, and its wonders appeared at every turn of the road.

But as with all fairy tales, there were aggravations, too. Some of them came in the form of trolls. Others came in the shape of dragons. The worst, though, were the carefully camouflaged pools of quicksand I found along the way, each so deep and dense I thought I'd never climb free. Fortunately, I had help. There were folks who cared enough to yank me out of the muck and the mire, point me in the right direction, and keep me going. Had it not been for their input, courage, and sense of conviction, this book would never have seen completion. To that end, I owe the following people more than just a simple vote of thanks. I owe them my undying gratitude.

To my dear friend and confidante, Linn Lipford, the Queen of the Chopping Block, who conjured this book in her mind's eye, pushed me to write it, and refused to give me one moment of peace until it was done.

To the Royal Court of New Page: Ron, Anne, Laurie, Jodi, Stacey, Kirsten, Jackie, and Briana, who waved magic wands and conjured powerful spells to get this book out on time, onto the shelves, and into your hands.

To Mike Lewis, the White Knight of acquisitions editors, who slew dragons at the speed of light, knocked ogres out of beanstalks, and obliterated every bridge-hugging troll along the way.

To my Fairy Godmother, Patricia Telesco, whose magic rendered an invitation to the ball of authorship, provided the golden coach that brought me there, and keeps me from falling flat on my face while waltzing through life.

To Sirona Knight, Sorceress Extraordinaire, whose bubbling cauldron of encouragement consistently dispels my fears and insecurities and bathes me in the warmth of true friendship.

To the incredibly captivating Prince of Yetis, A.J. Drew, whose zest for life, love of fun, and remarkable sense of personal generosity and friendship continues to inspire me along the personal path.

To murder mystery King, M.R. Sellars, a Prince Charming in his own right, whose constant friendship, words of encouragement, and long-distance hugs keep me going when I don't think I can.

To Sandi Liss, my favorite Princess Perfect, for her generosity in allowing me to use her conjuring story, for graciously perusing chapters, and for her ongoing support and friendship.

To Scott Appell, the charming Prince of the New York Horticultural Society, for lending his magical expertise and help in working out the details for the lust charms in this book.

Most of all, to The Dunigan Clan, whose sense of family is unsurpassed and whose appreciation for that which matters most—honor, integrity, and the true meaning of love—keeps me ever mindful that real princes and princesses are born every day.

Contents

Introduction

nce upon a time in a faraway land, there lived a young princess of incomparable beauty. Although she seemed to have everything a girl could want—friends, riches, servants, and so forth—she was absolutely miserable. She dreamed, you see, of meeting a prince one day—a handsome, charming young man who would fall madly in love with her, sweep her up onto his white horse, and take her far away to his castle. Together, they'd rule his land. She'd rule his heart. And of course, they'd live happily ever after.

It hadn't happened, though. And from the way things looked, it wasn't going to. Alas, the beautiful young princess was plagued with Frogs: those nasty, devilish creatures who followed her everywhere, all the while insisting that they were really handsome princes in disguise. All she had to do, they said, was pick them up, give them a kiss, and break the evil spell that kept them from their crowns. The princess thought it sounded simple enough, so she tried it a few times. For her trouble, she got nothing but slimy lips and a great distaste for everything green.

That being the case, the princess wasn't a bit surprised to find yet one more tiresome, amphibious creature hopping right into her lap on what otherwise might have been a perfectly beautiful summer evening.

"Gorgeous, elegant Lady," said he, "I once was a handsome prince who held the world in the palm of my hand. I had riches and land. I had a swift, white horse and lived in a castle on the hill."

The princess, who had heard it all before, just rolled her eyes heavenward and prompted him to get on with his spiel.

"If I had but just one kiss from your luscious red lips, I'd be forever returned to the strapping young specimen of masculinity I once was. And if you'll do me just this one favor," he continued, "I'll marry you and take you for my queen. We'll live with my mother in the castle, where I'll allow you to cook our meals, scrub our floors, wash our clothes, bear my children, and be forever grateful for all I've given you. And, of course, we'll live happily ever after."

The princess pondered his proposition. She turned it over and over in her mind. And then, as she sat down to a scrumptious meal of pearl onions in cream sauce and delicately sautéed frog legs, she clasped her hands in delight and said, "I don't froggin' think so!"

Granted, the princess went a bit far. But the point is that the very thought of not finding true love and romance makes us do crazy things. Why? Because they're the strongest driving forces in the human makeup. We dream of them. We hunger for them. Then we set off to search them out. Not just any old love will do, though. We set out to find the love of the century—something timeless and perfect, something that's able to cross all boundaries and overcome all obstacles—the same sort of something that made Cinderella and Prince

Charming so appealing. All we're looking for is that forever kind of love that makes our hearts pound 90-to-nothing and leaves us weak in the knees. Is that too much to ask?

More to the point, does it even exist?

Yes! And it's out there for everyone. The reason we don't find it, though, is because, unlike the princess, we're impatient. We're in a hurry and don't like to wait. So we talk ourselves into thinking that what we've found is the real thing. We settle for second best, and then we wake up one morning only to discover that Prince Charming—that gallant, handsome man who danced all night and rode the white horse—is really just a Frog in disguise.

So, what do we do? How do we disentangle ourselves? More important, how do we keep future Frogs from invading our lives and stealing our hearts?

Enchantments of the Heart not only answers these questions, but it also provides an easy-to-follow magical formula for finding the perfect love. Embroidered with spells, embellished with rituals, and tied with the ribbons of practical advice, it's all you'll ever need to find the love of your life, that timeless, romantic, delectable liaison guaranteed to leave you breathless, quivering, and begging for more. Yes, it's the one that squelches the most annoying sound in the world: the sound of "ribbit" in the morning!

—Dorothy Morrison
January 2002

A note to the reader

This book was written from my viewpoint: the viewpoint of a woman who was inundated with more Frogs than she could shake a stick at. In my case, the Frogs were men. This in no way is to say that Frogs are solely male. They definitely exist in the feminine gender as well to invade the lives of wonderful, worthwhile, trusting men all over the world.

That being the case, this book was also written for fabulous men everywhere, and the techniques described herein will also work well for finding Princess Perfect. All you need is an open mind and some serious application—and before you know it, she'll float right into your life. I guarantee it!

"Anything less than mad, passionate, extraordinary love is a complete and utter waste of time. There are already too many mediocre things in life—and love certainly shouldn't be one of them."

—Author unknown

Chapter One

The Cinderella Complex
and the
Snow White Syndrome

"So if there's really a Prince out there for everyone, then where the hell is mine?"

I eyed her from across the table. The despair in her voice matched the disgust on her face. And quietly, I remembered a time not long ago—a time when I'd sounded and looked much the same way.

"Well?!"

"If you really want to meet a Prince, you have to stay away from the pond."

The truth of the matter is that Prince Charming and Princess Perfect just don't frequent the same places that Frogs do. They stay away from the slime. They don't step in the muck. And they seldom—if ever—hop down to the pond. The fact is, if you truly want to meet a Prince or Princess, you have to stop frequenting those places, too.

In this case, the pond isn't a body of water. It's a breeding ground for Frogs and other unsavory characters. It includes singles bars, lonely-hearts clubs, and other places that we often think of as dating arenas. It also encompasses casinos, cocktail parties, support groups, and—this may surprise you—churches. Don't get me wrong: There's nothing wrong with any of those places. It's just that real royalty usually doesn't go there.

Instead, they go to normal everyday places: the grocery store, the Laundromat, the dry cleaners, the newsstand, the post office, and the mall. Occasionally, you may find them walking the dog or lounging about at the home of a mutual friend. But most likely, they're doing exactly what you're doing: sitting at home wondering why no one wants them.

The fact is, these folks aren't just nice people. They're *really* nice people, and this can cause a serious problem. Why? Because we have come to equate the word *nice* with the word *dull,* and the one thing we fear more than spending our lives alone is the prospect of spending it with someone who bores us. We don't just want excitement and adventure; we need it. We thrive on it. In fact, we live for it. And because of that, we usually opt for exciting types who provide lots of what we want but stomp on our hearts in the process. So, Prince Charming and Princess Perfect, no matter how wonderful they are, simply get left out of the loop. Finally, they just resign themselves to the fact that there's something wrong with them. And there they sit, disgusted, lonely, and dismayed.

If that's the case then, how do you ever find the perfect love?

Well, you don't—at least, not until you're ready. And you can't be ready until you love yourself, become your own best friend, and learn to be the best company you've ever had.

Now, before you start rolling your eyes, just hear me out. Loving yourself has nothing to do with being self-centered or arrogant. It has everything, however, to do with finding your perfect love. For starters, these types aren't interested in clingy, needy, high-maintenance mates. Why? Because they've already rescued Rapunzel, Cinderella, Snow White, and a bevy of other hand-wringers more times than they care to remember. What they're really looking for are strong, independent partners—partners who can handle whatever comes their way and who *want* them rather than *need* them. People who don't love themselves just don't fit the bill.

The Cinderella Complex

Sadly enough, most of us don't fit that bill—at least, not at first. But it's not our fault. It's all part of the Cinderella Complex: a nasty, societal brainwashing campaign designed to keep us in line—and, of course, turn us into a heap of sweet subservients that would rival even the most submissive group of Stepford wives. Here's how it works.

First, we're brainwashed into thinking that it's our job to carry the weight of the world. And as natural nurturers, fixers, and peacekeepers, we jump at the chance. Then once we're fully engrossed in the challenge, the real fun begins. We start to believe that we exist solely to nurture everybody on the planet and that it's our job to bolster egos, pick up the pieces when they shatter, and, of course, make the world a better place to live. It's not long before we're catering to every whim, striving to make every wish come true, and doing it with a smile bright enough to outshine the sun. It's a much larger feat than even the most practiced Fairy Godmother could manage. But we do it. We have to. After all, we think that it's the sole reason for our existence.

That being the case, there's no time left to nurture ourselves. Even if there were, though, we'd probably just ditch the idea. Why? Because ever since we emerged from the womb, we've been conditioned to believe that our own needs aren't important. That to pamper ourselves is selfish. And that if we even so much as think about it, all hell will break loose and life as we know it will cease to exist. The end result is that we retreat to the dustbin and roll in the ashes. We become needy, unhappy people, folks who hunger for the slightest compliment, the scarcest shred of interest, and the most miniscule show of affection. With that in mind, it's no wonder that we wind up with Frogs!

Fortunately, the Cinderella Complex doesn't have to be all-consuming. That's because there's a tiny voice in each of us that begs to buck the system and screams to break free. We can stop the complex dead in its tracks. All we have to do is hear the voice and take action. It's not that hard—especially once we begin to see things as they really are. Sometimes, though, we need some help. In my case, it was delivered with a firm hand.

I had just undergone a nasty divorce. My confidence was shattered. My ego was ripped to shreds. And to make matters worse, I felt useless, fat, ugly, and stupid. It wasn't a pretty picture, but no matter what I did, I just couldn't seem to pull myself out of the muck and get it together. So I just sat there day in and day out, praying to be swallowed by the mire and delivered of my misery.

Fortunately, my good friend, Chuck, had other plans.

He arrived at my apartment one afternoon, camera in hand. When I finally opened the door, he just shoved me aside and barged right in.

"Get dressed." It was an order, not a request.

"I don't feel…"

"I don't care what you feel like. Get dressed. Put on some makeup. And for God's sake, do something with that hair, unless, of course, you want me to start snapping this shutter right now!"

I opened my mouth again, but it was too late. He'd already turned on the shower and was coming toward me with the speed of a mad bull.

"Get in the shower. Or I swear, Dorothy, I'll toss you in myself."

Of course, I was furious. No one had ever spoken to me like that. I set my jaw and crossed my arms. I assumed my most stubborn you-can't-make-me attitude. But it was no use: Chuck wasn't to be trifled with, and before I knew it, I was not only clean, dressed, made up, and coifed, but out the door and in his car.

You see, Chuck was a man with a mission. And though he definitely cared about my well-being, my attitude problems were just a small part of things. He was an amateur photographer in need of photos— photos good enough to win him a spot in the state fair competition. The gist of it was that he couldn't have photos without a model, and it was my lucky day. We spent the rest of the day at the park, with Chuck incessantly snapping away and capturing my every move and mood.

Three hours later, he was still at it. I was worn out, exhausted, and sick to death of the bossy man who constantly interrupted my every sentence with orders: *"smile," "tilt your head," "look to the right,"* and *"keep your hands away from your face."* Finally, I just burst into tears. Of course, he captured that, too.

"Cry if you want," he chirped happily, *"but you'll thank me later."* Then he had the audacity to laugh.

I wasn't just pissed. I was livid. I wanted to slap him until his teeth rattled. Choke him until his eyes bulged. Chew him up and spit him out, then toss him from my life like yesterday's garbage. I didn't dare, though. He'd have gotten pictures of that, too. Instead,

I just treated him to a dose of silence that lasted all the way home.

That didn't deter him, though. In fact, he had the nerve to show up at my door again three days later. This time, he had a huge package wrapped in brown paper.

"Go away." I said it with enough ice to make hell freeze over, but, Chuck being Chuck, he just brushed me aside like so much lint and marched right into my living room. He tossed the package on the table. Then he went about the business of removing everything from my walls.

"What the hell are you doing?! This is my house! I won't allow you to…"

"Just can it!"

Then he ripped open the package and the contents spilled out. I couldn't believe my eyes. Scattered across the floor lay 30 or 40 black-and-white photographs of me—each one enlarged to the whopping dimensions of 16 by 20 inches. Before I could stop him, he'd tacked them up all over my apartment.

"Now then," he said with a grin, *"close your windows, lock your doors, and turn off your phone. No TV. No reading. No outside entertainment of any kind. At least, not for a week."*

"What?!"

"Just do it, Dorothy. It's time you learned who you really are. Get to know yourself. Become your own best friend. Who knows? You might even come to love yourself a little."

I'm still not sure exactly why, but I took Chuck's advice. I have to admit, though, that it was more than just a little disconcerting, for no matter where I went, there I was—literally bigger than life—gazing down on myself from the walls, looking up at myself from the couch, and even staring at myself from the refrigerator door. How much of oneself can one take? It definitely took some getting used to.

Finally, as a measure of self-preservation, I began to see the pictures not as reflections of myself, but as mirrors of an entirely different person: someone I hadn't met, didn't know, and could be absolutely objective about. And as I did, a sort of unconventional therapy began to flow. I studied the moods, the tilt of the head, the quizzical arch of the right eyebrow, the crooked smile that found symmetry in laughter. Most of all, though, I studied the eyes—the mirrors of the soul. In their fleeting changes—from joy to anger, from whimsy to reflection—I rediscovered something that I thought was lost forever: a firm grasp of the person within and a fondness for the person without. It was definitely a turning point in my life, for on that day, I rediscovered personal compassion—and in doing so, I rediscovered myself.

Chuck's "therapy" not only worked wonders for me, but it reminded me of some important things I'd forgotten along my way. For one thing, complete subservience to another human being is more than just emotionally harmful. It is the absolute key to self-destruction. Even worse, it gets us nowhere in the love and romance department. This doesn't mean that we shouldn't compromise from time to time. We should. What it does mean, though, is that we shouldn't lose ourselves in the process. We have the right to personal opinion, the right to disagree, and the right to say no if something makes us uncomfortable. Anything short of that crushes personal creativity, which is the very thing that sets us apart as individuals.

Another thing I remembered is that there is no way on Earth that we can truly tend to anyone else until we learn to nurture ourselves. Why? Because if we don't know how to meet our own needs, we're missing the basics. We have no point of reference. This means that we spend tons of time and energy trying to make everyone feel special. Because we really don't have a clue, we spend even more time and energy second-guessing ourselves. Even worse, no one—not even the object of our affections—is happy. It's more than just a no-win situation: It's an effort in futility.

That brings up another point: True happiness has nothing to do with what we can do for other people. Instead, it has everything to do with how we feel about ourselves. It comes from being proud of who we are, how far we've traveled, and what we've become. It comes from a spot way down inside ourselves—a spot so deep, so raw, and so hidden that only we can touch it. Sadly, until we begin to see ourselves as the deserving, valuable, and worthwhile people we are, there's a good chance that we—the only people in the world capable of delivering that all-consuming personal happiness that we seek—may just come up empty-handed.

I don't want to live like that. Do you?

Crushing the Complex

Not everyone has a friend like Chuck, but that's okay. His style of treatment just isn't necessary for most folks. What *is* necessary is a good, solid remedy. A program of sorts that's easy to follow, yet so powerful that it works even despite human stubbornness and doubt. To that end, I've devised such a plan. It involves just three easy steps. Once you've taken them, you'll not only see yourself in a different light but be well on your way to becoming your own best friend. Guaranteed.

Step 1: The "I am Valuable" Ritual

Unlike most rituals, you can successfully perform this one regardless of moon phase, day of the week, or your frame of mind. Even a bad attitude won't mar its effectiveness. The only things necessary for successful results are 15 minutes of quiet time on six consecutive days and three candles (one white, one pink, and one purple). The ritual itself will take care of the rest.

Start by taking a deep breath and clearing your mind. Light the white candle and say:

> I am valuable and bright
> I am power, strength, and might
> I am most deserving of
> The simplest, truest form of love
> The very love that I wish for
> The love that lives within my core
> The love that flows so easily
> The one I shower endlessly
> On the others in my life
> Without regard to my own strife
> So...

Light the pink candle and say:

> Today, I make this vow
> From this time forward I'll allow
> My true self to be enveloped
> Nurtured, cared for, and developed
> By the warmth of love I hold
> Never-ending, strong and bold
> And...

Light the purple candle and say:

> Because I do deserve
> All the good life has to serve
> I'll accept its gifts with joy
> And each delight I shall enjoy
> Without worry, without shame
> Without selflessness or blame
> For I am valuable and rare
> I deserve the best of care

Allow the candles to burn for 15 minutes before extinguishing them. Repeat the ritual daily for the next five days, letting the candles burn down completely on the sixth day.

Step 2: Scrubbing the Dustbin

You can begin this process at any time during Step 1, but it isn't necessary. What is imperative, though, is that no time lapses between the end of Step 1 and the beginning of Step 2. For that reason, begin this step no later than the seventh day of the program.

Because Step 2 only involves getting rid of what we don't need or can't use anymore, this should be the easiest step of the entire program. However, it's often the most difficult. That's because we, as human beings, have more than just a slight affinity for possessions. It's not our fault, though; somewhere along the line we got the idea that whoever winds up with the most toys wins. We go about our lives craving, bargaining, and collecting. In fact, we base a large portion of our self-worth upon what we acquire. It never occurs to us that there's really no prize at the end of the line, so we just keep at it, and before long, our homes are filled with so much stuff that we can hardly kick a path to the proverbial door.

Unfortunately, this sort of thinking also spills over into our spiritual and emotional worlds. We tend to collect hurt feelings, wounded pride, and other painful things—things that should have been dealt with immediately and tossed away like yesterday's garbage. We allow them to fester, increase in size, and gain momentum until they're no longer the minute sets of triviality they were at the onset. They become real, live, breathing, eye-blinking monsters who rear their ugly heads and have us for lunch. Of course, we have no one to blame but ourselves.

What does all this have to do with crushing the Cinderella Complex? Everything! Although it's nice to have clean physical and emotional houses, getting rid of our rubbish goes further than that. We can't make way for the new and wonderful if the old and useless are taking up all the space. But more important than that, this process begins the demolition phase of the dustbin—that place where we go to wring our hands, belittle ourselves, and wallow in self-pity. That place where Frogs breed, where royalty seldom treads, and where matches for glass slippers are only found in fairy tales. That said, grab an assortment of boxes or garbage bags and let's get started!

The Ritual

This ritual doesn't have an exact time frame. It depends solely on how quickly you work and how much clutter you have lying around. For that reason, this step could take a few days, a few weeks, or even a few months. How long it takes is not important, though. What is important is that you see each item thrown away as part of what's keeping you from having the happiness you deserve.

Begin this ritual by taking a few deep breaths and clearing your mind. Then, without any further thought, dig in immediately. Otherwise, you'll never get this done.

The Clothes Closet

The goal here is to reduce your clothing by two-thirds. Tough? You bet. Unthinkable? Not really. Just start with the following guidelines. If you're in doubt about something and/or it doesn't fit a category listed, just grit your teeth and toss it out. You'll be glad you did!

- ᴄʒ **It's out of style.** So what if you can still wear it? You won't (not even around the house!). Throw it out.

- ᴄʒ **It doesn't fit.** Even if your weight fluctuates, will it still be in style when you're able to wear it? Probably not. Throw it away.

- ᴄʒ **It has sentimental value.** It really doesn't matter if it was your first prom dress, or if your first love thought it made you look stunning, or if you wore it on your wedding day. Those relationships are dead and gone. So are these clothes. Throw them away.

- ଔ **It doesn't hang right.** Outfits that make you look like a horse (or feel like one) only damage your self-esteem. Chuck it immediately!

- ଔ **It hasn't been worn in more than a year.** If you haven't had it on in the last 12 months, it's just taking up valuable space. Throw it away.

- ଔ **It's old and worn-out, but it's your favorite.** Oh, *please!* Would you really want a Prince or Princess to see you in *that*? Or even worse, the Queen Mother? Toss it out!

- ଔ **While you're in the closet,** take a good look at anything you may have stored in there (old love letters, pictures of old flames, and the like). Take one last look if you must, but know that keeping them around will only crush your self-confidence and keep you from having what you deserve. Complete the closure by tossing them in the trash—or, if you're really feeling sassy, by setting them on fire. [Use extreme caution when burning anything. Always use a fireproof container and keep a watchful eye on items until all flames are extinguished.]

Once the closet is clean, you'll begin to feel as if the weight of the world has just been lifted from your shoulders. That's the good news. The bad news is that you may feel as if you've nothing left to wear. If that thought creeps in, just push it aside—for at least 30 days. If you still feel the same way when the month is up, then splurge a little and go shopping. Don't purchase anything—no matter how good the bargain—unless it fits, it hangs right, and you look absolutely stunning in it. After all, you deserve to look stunning—anything less is beneath you!

The Linen Closet

This is an area that most folks never think to clean. Why? Because to their way of thinking, sheets and towels just don't wear out. Although that may be true, changes are often necessary because of lifestyle and/or emotional attachment. Think I'm kidding? I once kept a favorite set of sheets for 10 years, even though I never slept well on them. They reminded me of an old flame, a love who had died just after I bought them.

At any rate, old linens (even towels) do carry heavy emotional attachments. For that reason, get rid of anything that doesn't make you smile. Because these items can be relatively expensive, though, you may not be able to toss your whole assortment. In that case, just throw out what you can afford to replace now, and replace the rest of your collection as finances allow.

One last word of advice: Buy a special set of sheets and put it aside. You'll need it when you find the love of your life!

The following represent good rules of thumb for clearing out the linen closet. Throw it away if:

- ᘓ It's torn, thin, or frayed.

- ᘓ It reminds you of someone who is no longer in your life.

- ᘓ The color or pattern no longer reflects your personality.

Kitchen Cabinets, Pantry, and Refrigerator

These are other areas that we seldom think to clear, but they're just as important as the others. Why? Because the kitchen and it's related areas comprise the heart of the home. As silly as it sounds, its contents make us feel loved and nurtured. The aroma of baking bread, for example, conveys a happy, childlike feeling, and the smell of spaghetti sauce makes us feel warm and secure. That being the case, it's imperative that any area affecting the emotions with such force be cleared immediately of negative energy. The following guidelines will help you get started:

- ◌ॐ **Plastics.** If it's stained, misshapen, or missing its lid, toss it out. The same goes for extra margarine or sherbet containers. (You really have no use for more than five, do you?)

- ◌ॐ **Pots and pans.** Throw away anything that's missing a handle. Likewise, throw away items with burned bottoms or shredded inner coatings.

- ◌ॐ **Dishes.** Chuck anything that's chipped, cracked, or useless—regardless of sentimental value. If you favor hot drinks in large mugs, you have no use for small cups. Get rid of them as well.

- ◌ॐ **Food items.** Toss everything that's out-of-date. The same goes for any canned goods or freezer items that you haven't used in a year.

Closing the Ritual

Materials list:

    1 black candle
    1 brown candle
    1 white candle
    Large metal cookie sheet
    Box of table salt
    Paper
    Pen

Once all the aforementioned areas are cleared of
unnecessary items, gather your materials and spread
them out on the kitchen counter. Place the cookie sheet
in a horizontal position and arrange the candles, beginning at the far left side of the pan, in the following
order: black, brown, and white. Draw a salt circle (ap-
proximately three inches in diameter) on the right side
of the pan. Use the salt to draw an arrow extending
from the white candle to the salt circle. Then write the
following words on the paper:

> All that is good
> All that is joyful
> All that is personally beneficial

Fold the paper into thirds, then into thirds again,
and place it inside the salt circle. Light the black
candle and say:

> I name you for both hurt and pain
> And that which keeps me from the gain
> Of everything that I deserve
> No more chaos shall you serve

Visualize the black candle turning into brown.
Then light the brown candle and say:

> I name you for the transformation
> Of all that brings me consternation
> And as I light you, things will turn
> Around for me—flame dance and burn

Visualize the brown candle turning into white. Then
light the white candle and say:

> I name you for what's good and sweet
> A metamorphosis complete
> That clears poor energy away
> And brings me what I ask this day

Follow the arrow with your eyes and gaze upon the paper in the center of the circle. Say with fervor and feeling:

> The best in life is mine
> Opportunities unwind
> All the pieces fit in place
> With perfect ease and perfect grace
> A charmed life, I now do live
> And I grab all it has to give

Let the candles burn completely out, then collect the salt, paper, and any remaining wax in a zippered plastic bag. On the next dark moon, dig a hole in the ground. Bury the contents of the bag and throw the bag away.

Step 3: The Pampering Ritual

Regardless of how many times you remind yourself of your personal value and worth, nothing good is going to come from it until you truly believe that you deserve the best life has to offer. And you're not going to truly believe that until you see yourself as important enough to do something about it. Take the first step. Maybe even go as far as to—gasp!—do something nice for yourself. This is the reason for the Pampering Ritual.

This ritual gives us an excuse to do that wonderful thing for ourselves that we'd ordinarily never even dream of. And we need that excuse. Why? Because we're conditioned to believe that pampering ourselves is tantamount to embracing the height of selfishness, and we just can't seem to get past this notion. But we'll never get anything good in life until we do.

Begin this ritual by making a list of things that make you feel pampered. These don't have to be expensive activities; they can be anything at all. Some ideas might include a manicure or pedicure, a candlelight bubble bath complete with a glass of wine, a bouquet of flowers on the table, or even silk lingerie. (My personal favorite is a coffeemaker in the bedroom!) The only restriction here is that your list be comprised of things you wouldn't normally indulge in—and the more decadent, the better.

Once the page is full, pick one of the entries. Then take the appropriate action (schedule the appointment, place the order, make the preparations, or whatever) to make it happen. Just before indulging in the activity itself, though, give yourself the go-ahead by saying the following words—and meaning them:

> There's no one else on Earth like me
> I'm a unique exercise in creativity
> I am wonderful—I am rare
> I deserve the richest fare
> That is offered on this plane
> I accept it without guilt or shame

Then follow through and have fun. Repeat this ritual at least once each month, using another activity from your list. Continue until all the activities are crossed off your list.

The Snow White Syndrome

Although the Cinderella Complex is definitely a tough adversary, there's nothing in this world that rears its head as nastily as the Snow White Syndrome. And when we find them coupled together—which is more often than not—they don't just damage our self-worth: They actually make us want to stay in bed, pull the covers over our heads, and refuse to face the world. That's because the Snow White Syndrome attacks the way we look. And even though society would have us believe otherwise, that's something over which we have very little control.

The problem is that we all believe we should fit into a certain mold. Of course, our personal gene pools don't allow such folly. But still we strive to emulate the beautiful people on billboards, in magazine ads, and on the silver screen. We diet till we faint. We exercise till we drop. We don't fit the bill, but that doesn't stop us. It doesn't even slow us down. Somewhere in the back of our little pea-brains, we truly believe that if we work hard enough and continue on a course of deprivation, we will finally—someday—fit into the size 3 of our dreams.

We won't. Not today. Not tomorrow. Not ever.

Sadly, all we have to show for our trouble is a troubled mind and a good case of personal animosity. We collapse to the floor in a crumpled heap and hide in the corner, weak, hungry, and sick. We hate the body that won't comply with our idea of beautiful. But we don't stop there. We hate ourselves, too. We just know that if we'd been more disciplined and less self-serving, we would have met our goals. Of course it's not true, but that doesn't matter.

Things get worse from that point. Our minds run amok. They work overtime, questioning this, questioning that—and before we know it, we're well on the way to a full-blown tizzy. Finally, we leap from the floor and rush to the mirror only to come face-to-face with our greatest fear: an image too awful, too ugly, and too disgusting for even the toughest mother on the planet to love. It's not really there, but that doesn't matter, either. Tears begin to fall, and the Snow White Syndrome is well on its way to victory.

I'm no stranger to this vicious enemy. In fact, we did battle not long ago. As is the norm, it waited until I wasn't looking, then slithered forth and attacked my point of least resistance: my weight.

I couldn't get into my clothes. It happened gradually, so at first I didn't believe it. I honestly thought I'd left the clothes in the dryer too long. Then I tried on some outfits that hadn't seen the dryer in months. I couldn't wear them either. I was appalled. I threw myself onto the bed and cried like a baby.

Then the real damage began. I took a trip down memory lane. I recalled how awful it was to be a fat child—not just any fat child, mind you, but the fat baby sister of fashion models and beauty queens. I remembered how insignificant I'd felt when introduced to others as the child with "personality." I remembered how, after that, nothing I accomplished— not good grades, not writing awards, not even drama kudos—had seemed to make any difference. My heart raced. Panic set in. I sobbed and wept and screamed. I threw the biggest hissy fit ever known to humankind.

Finally, a shred of common sense grabbed hold. I dried my tears and remembered a great diet I'd tried once. It was a wonderful program. I'd used it years ago to drop 40 pounds and managed to keep the weight off for more than a decade. It was tried-and-true. And because I only needed to lose 10 pounds in this case, they'd be gone in nothing flat. At least, that's what I thought. I was wrong.

The diet didn't work. No matter what I did—and believe me, I tried everything from counting fat grams to drinking tons of water to eating special food combinations—the pounds simply would not budge. Then to add insult to injury, I began to gain more weight. Panic returned. Worry set in. I was right back to that awful state of feeling fat, useless, and ugly. And try as I might, there didn't seem to be a darned thing I could do about it.

Slaughtering the Syndrome

Fortunately, solid information yanked me off the pity pot. I discovered that metabolisms (like taste buds) change every few years. The same goes for other body functions and mechanisms. No amount of physical exercise or food deprivation will ever completely resolve the problem. That being the case, adjustments were necessary—and they had to begin with my attitude.

Personal attitude is the only way to fully beat this syndrome. That's often easier said than done. We have years of brainwashing to unravel, scads of societal expectation to crush, and loads of emotional trash to discard. And no matter what we've been led to believe, we have to learn to love our bodies as they are—flaws included. That's a pretty hefty order, but there is a solution.

Step 1: Only the Facts

It starts with looking at the facts. This isn't always easy, though, because our minds tend to wander. Bits and pieces of former conditioning creep in, and before we know it we're bombarded with painful memories. We start to falter, and the syndrome attacks again with a well-placed jab. It's hard to stay on track.

For this reason, a few of my favorite carved-in-stone facts are listed here. Look at them as they are: cold, hard, and finite. See them without variance. Don't just peruse them. Commit them to memory. Whenever your mind resumes its conjuring game—and it will—recite them to yourself firmly and without question. By doing so, you'll lose the personal hold of the syndrome and knock it on its ass. And while it's down, you can get a jab in, too!

ℭℬ **Fact One:** Mirrors, because they are made of a fairly poor grade of glass, distort our reflections. Thus, we never see ourselves as we really are; only other people do. That being the case, we are truly much more beautiful than we think.

ℭℬ **Fact Two:** No one—not even the most gorgeous Hollywood star—is ever completely satisfied with the way he or she looks. We *all* think we're too fat, too thin, too short, too tall, too anything else you can imagine.

ℭℬ **Fact Three:** No one—unless he or she has had plastic surgery—has a perfectly symmetrical body or face. In fact, close examination proves that one side of *every* body is larger than the other.

ℭℬ **Fact Four:** Marilyn Monroe was a size 16, a size that, by today's standards, is reserved for the semi-obese. Yet no one ever thought of her as fat.

ℭℬ **Fact Five:** John Wayne was not nearly as large as he appeared on screen. He didn't even measure 6 feet tall, and his boot size was barely an 8.

- ের **Fact Six:** If we were truly built like Barbie or Ken dolls, our internal organs wouldn't function properly. In fact, we'd probably just have to do without some of them. Why? There simply wouldn't be enough body mass to house them.

- ের **Fact Seven:** Personal DNA and gene pool not only control the facial features, but the size, shape, and dimension of the body as well. This means that we have no control over the size of our frames and very little over the mass that covers them.

- ের **Fact Eight:** Gravity isn't selective. It hits all of us. This means that if we live long enough, we'll all have sagging breasts, butts, and bellies. No amount of personal deprivation or exercise will ever make it cease and desist. It's just part of life.

Step 2: Loving Your Body

This is the most important thing you'll ever do for yourself, but it's also the most difficult to take seriously. Why? Because it entails whispering sweet nothings, tender caresses, and general courtship. If this were a romantic partner we were talking about, there wouldn't be a problem. It's not, though; in this case, your body is the object of your affections.

At this point, I can almost see that peculiar expression creeping across your face. Before you decide that I've completely lost my mind, though, just hear me out. If you don't learn to love your body—and treat it with the same amount of tender loving care that you'd shower on some romantic interest—you're just asking for trouble. Here's why: Your body does more for you than any other mechanism on this planet. It houses and protects your internal organs. It filters out toxins so you don't get sick. It tells you when it's time to eat and sleep and gives you the ability to think, speak, and hear. If that's not enough, it also takes you wherever you want to go. Your body is a much better friend to you than any other you've ever had.

Sadly enough, though, most of us despise our bodies. Instead of seeing them as our best friends—and the most vital part of our physical existence—we see them as useless, cumbersome shapes that keep us from getting what we want. Of course, that's just ridiculous. More to the point, it's not true.

We are the ones who keep us from getting what we want. And we do it by not loving our bodies or ourselves—instead of the other way around. We decide that we're too fat or too thin. We decide that no one could love us with the body that we have. We decide that if we just had something more shapely, more willowy, or more muscular, we'd be fighting the royalty off with a stick. And with that sort of an attitude, Prince Charming and Princess Perfect never have a chance. Why? Because we're so deeply immersed in Frog cover that they can't even find us.

The fact is that beauty is in the eye of the beholder. Although that sounds old and trite, it's true. Take me, for example. I will never—no matter how hard I try—fit into the clothes of a runway model. My frame is large, my bones are big, and according to standardized height and weight charts, I am at least 25 pounds overweight. Yet, even back in high school when I weighed 200 pounds, I never lacked a date on Saturday night.

What was my secret? It was twofold, actually. First, I knew that members of the opposite sex all saw beauty differently. Large, shapely women appealed to some. Others were more attracted to wispier types. I knew that there was someone out there for everyone and that size and shape didn't matter.

Second, I was comfortable with my body. That being the case, I was a happy person and a lot of fun to be around. Because my weight and size weren't issues for me, they weren't issues for anyone else, either. In fact, no one even seemed to notice. All they saw was the fun-loving teenager who blossomed from the inside out. I kid you not, folks. I dated some of the most popular boys in school, always had mums for the football games, and never lacked a date for a single prom or homecoming dance—and all of it came from a positive attitude.

It's time to form a solid, loving relationship with your body. It's time to grab some sass and don a new attitude. If you don't, you'll still be inundated with Frogs, and you'll never find your perfect love. It's as simple as that. So wipe that funny look off your face and let's get started!

The Love-My-Body Ritual

Begin this ritual by picking up the phone. Make an appointment for a manicure and pedicure. (Don't scoff, gentlemen. This is for you, too!) If you can't get in for a week or two, don't worry. Just schedule the appointment and remember to keep it.

Once that's done, grab a candle and some incense (any color or scent will do) and head for the bathroom. Run a tub of hot water and add your favorite bath oil or bubble bath. Then undress, light the candle and incense, and step in.

Lie back in the tub and close your eyes. Relax every part of your body. Begin with your toes, your feet, your ankles, and your legs. Work your way up to your hips, stomach, chest, shoulders, and arms. Pay close attention to your neck. Turn it from side to side, and roll it in both clockwise and counterclockwise directions. Sink further down into the water, and feel its warmth caressing your body into total relaxation. Clear your mind and savor the warm luxury of liquid peace and serenity.

After a few moments, liberally apply your favorite soap to a bath sponge. Slowly lather every part of your body, searching out each nook and cranny. Do this deliberately and tenderly, as if you were bathing the love of your life. Relish the feeling of the sponge's silky lather as it floats across your skin.

Afterward, carefully rinse the soap away with warm water and pat dry. Apply petroleum jelly or baby oil to your feet, knees, elbows, and other areas that have become rough and dry from neglect. Then slowly smooth on your favorite body lotion. Gently massage it into your skin until all traces disappear. As you massage, know that you are caring for the most precious gift you'll ever receive and a friend who will be with you for the rest of your life.

Finally, stand in front of a full-length mirror. Look at your body. Know that it is formed in the image of the Creator/ix, that it is the body of Deity, and that it is perfect in every way. Then look into the eyes of your reflection and say:

> I am the God/dess! I am S/He
> Who creates the world I see
> Each thing of beauty, charm, and grace
> Each perfect time—each perfect place
> I am God/dess! I am S/He
> Who brings to life reality

Then wrap your arms around yourself in a big hug
and say:

> I love you, Body, as you are
> You are perfect by and far
> A perfect shape—a perfect friend
> I'll love you till our days do end

Repeat this ritual weekly or whenever the Snow
White Syndrome tries to rear her ugly head.

For the Ladies Only

Once you've made friends with your body, it's time for a
little enhancement magic. That's right, ladies: It's time to
dig out the makeup bag!

Don't roll your eyes or try to make excuses by saying that
makeup is a cop-out. It just won't work here. Why? Because
enhancing your body is just the same as enhancing any other
personal magic. You wouldn't think twice, for example, about
adding some oomph to a prosperity spell, a ritual for good
health, or an effort to find a new job. That being the case,
it's just good sense not to skimp here, either.

If you're still not sure, consider the wisdom of the Fairy
Godmother. She knew that if Cinderella arrived at the ball
without a few enhancements, Prince Charming would never
give her a second glance. They'd never dance all night.
They'd never fall in love. And the glass slipper search would
never have come into play. By incorporating this tiny bit of
magic in the wave of her wand, though, she was easily able to
choreograph the most romantic event in fairy-tale history—
all because she had the good sense to add some necessary
accoutrements.

Here's the deal: If you look like a scullery maid, you'll feel like one. And scullery maids, regardless of how kind or caring or wonderful they are, just don't attract Prince Charming. Why? Because they simply don't have the poise and self-confidence necessary to catch his eye.

Take that same scullery maid and apply a little makeup. Her confidence levels rise. She dons a new attitude. Heads turn, and people on the street take notice. No matter what she looked like or how she felt when she climbed out of bed that morning, she now feels like royalty. And because she feels like royalty, the rest of the world views her that way, too. It's as simple as that.

So do yourself a favor and take a cue from the Fairy Godmother. Find your makeup bag and give it a good dusting. Then resolve to spend 15 minutes every morning using what's inside. You may not need much. A dab of lipstick, a bit of mascara, and a touch of blush may do the trick. But make no mistake: No matter how few the necessary enhancements, the 15 minutes you spend with that makeup bag will bring you more results than you ever imagined. You'll not only walk away looking and feeling like a Princess, but you'll draw the respect and notice that every Princess deserves—guaranteed.

For the Men Only

Although you're not apt to be dusting off a makeup bag, there's no reason you can't spruce up a bit and appear more princely. The same logic mentioned in the section for the ladies applies to men as well. If you look like a Prince, you feel like a Prince. And if you feel like a Prince, others treat you in kind. Let's get started.

We all know that some things make us look and feel scruffy—and for men, it's usually the lack of a good razor. Don't get me wrong: There's nothing wrong with beards. In fact, lots of women love them. It's just that if you're going to sport facial hair, it needs grooming and trimming on a regular basis. If you're not the bearded type, you need to take a few minutes to shave every day. Either way, good grooming goes a long way toward looking princely.

Another thing to keep in mind is the condition of your hands. Guffaw if you want, but there's nothing less appealing to women than dirty fingernails or rough hands. Just a few minutes spent with a nail brush and some antibacterial soap easily solve the problem. After they're clean, rub a little petroleum jelly into your hands. Rough, dry skin is only a memory, and you're good to go.

The last bit of advice here has to do with your clothes. Their type or style isn't important. What *does* matter is that they're clean and unwrinkled. No matter how wonderful you are, Princess Perfect won't look twice if you appear to have slept in your clothes for a week.

The Beauty Spell

Contrary to popular belief, the best time to perform magic is *not* when things are bad. Instead, it's much more effective to call on the universe when everything is going so well that you almost can't believe it. Why? Because you want things to continue moving in that direction. The last thing you need is a fly in the ointment or some set of complications getting in the way, and some magical help is the best preventative measure I know.

Such is the reason for the following spell. You look like royalty. You feel like royalty. And there's just no reason to invite trouble. That being the case, gather your materials and prepare to work this spell when Friday rolls around. You'll be glad you did!

Materials list:

1 de-stemmed red or pink rose bud
[Note to men: Use 1 tsp. dried
lavender instead of the rose]
1 pink candle
1 bottle witch hazel
6 cotton balls
1 4-inch-square cheesecloth or fine net
tulle
1 6-inch-long pink ribbon
1 pint-sized glass jar with a screw-on lid

Pull the cotton balls apart and wrap them around the rosebud so that it's completely covered. Then place the wrapped bud in the center of the cheesecloth or tulle, gather the fabric ends, and secure them with the ribbon. Hold the bundle in your hand and squeeze it firmly several times (this bruises the bud and helps to release its essential oils), then place it in the jar. Add the witch hazel, secure the lid, and shake well.

Light the candle and place the jar in front of it. Then place your hands over the jar and invoke Venus, the goddess of beauty, by saying:

> Lovely Venus, Beauteous One
> Lend power to what I've begun
> Bless this potion with your grace
> And bring to me a lovely face

Leave the jar in front of the candle until it extinguishes itself. Apply the lotion to clean, dry skin, using the "bundle" as an applicator.

Chapter Two

From Frogs to Princes

Frogs no longer have to jump in my lap—or give me that evil sorcerer song and dance—before I know who they are. I can spot one from a mile off. It wasn't always that way, though. I had to live a life simply inundated with them before I got a clue. Unless you know what you're looking for, that could happen to you, too.

Froggie Comes A 'Courtin'

Fortunately, some Frogs are obvious ribbiters: habitual gamblers, chronic substance abusers, thieves, axe murderers, and those with a history of physical violence—and you'll know to stay away from them. Others aren't so transparent. They don't show their true colors until they've got you hooked. Then it's too late, at least for your heart.

Such is the case with the following Frogs. (Please note: The word *he* is used throughout this section for the sake of continuity only and is in no way meant to constitute sexism. Feel free to exchange the gender-specific words in this text for those that apply to you personally.) Learn the list. Commit it to memory. And whatever you do, don't let them into your life. Once there, removing them is harder than pulling hens' teeth!

The Victim

We all have an inherent need to feel necessary. And this is how the Victim reels you in. He not only needs you, but he needs you more desperately than anyone else on Earth. He allows you to run his life by remote control and is perfectly willing to do whatever you say will fix it.

He's charming, grateful, and attentive. You're happy, he's happy, and life is good—at least for a while.

The problem with the Victim is that no matter what you do, it's never enough. Someone always has it in for him. Someone's always screwing with him. Someone's always passing him over. There's just no end. Of course, it never occurs to him that he may be at fault somehow or that the crux of the real problem lies within himself.

The Schmoozer

Although the Schmoozer is a first cousin of the Victim, he really doesn't need for you to fix anything. He handles his life with the grace and ease of a man in complete control. In fact, there's nothing he can't do. Best of all, he always manages to get everything done in short order. Don't breathe a sigh of relief, yet, though. The Schmoozer is still a Frog, and it shows in his methodology!

The reason that he always manages to get things done is because he knows how to delegate. He makes his every project sound so great that you can hardly wait to see the results. Then once he sees the excitement in your eyes, he magnanimously invites you to be a part of things. He outlines the project, shows you what needs to be done, and gets you engrossed in the job. Five minutes later, he's nowhere to be found. You're doing all the work, and the Schmoozer is off having fun!

The Guilt Freak

This Frog always has a large assortment of projects in the works. He has grandiose ideas and he likes to see them materialize. Unlike the Schmoozer, though, the Guilt Freak is always more than willing to roll up his sleeves, get dirty, and help with the work at hand. The only catch is that when things don't turn out as planned, he's never even partially at fault. All the blame—every single bit of it—falls solely on you! If you had done this or hadn't done that, things would have been different. Things would have been wonderful. Everything would have been just as he'd envisioned it at the onset. And before it's said and done, you find yourself believing it.

The User

A well-mannered charmer with excellent taste, this Frog has an innate feel for the luxurious, the expensive, and the rare and wonderful. He not only takes you out on the town, wines and dines you at extravagant restaurants, and reserves tickets for your favorite cultural events, but he is perfectly delighted to do so. He's genteel and chivalrous. He lavishes you with praise. In fact, you couldn't find a better date— except for one thing: The User is always short of cash. Sometimes he even forgets to bring his wallet. You wind up paying for everything, and before you know it you owe your soul to American Express!

The Overachiever

Though it's possible to find this Frog anywhere, he is usually a person of professional status, such as a physician, attorney, or entrepreneur. He works hard for a living. He knows important people. He makes tons of money, and he doesn't mind spending it on you. In fact, life with this Frog is filled with expensive gifts, an unlimited checking account, and platinum credit cards.

So what's the problem? There isn't one—if you like spending your life alone. The Overachiever never has time for you, and even when he does, he's never truly there. His beeper or cell phone always takes priority. First, it's just a dinner or vacation. After a while, though, it even interrupts your sex life. And there you sit, so angry, unsatisfied, and miserable, that all the diamonds in the world won't make the slightest bit of difference.

The Big Cheese

Although he's closely related to the Overachiever, this Frog isn't nearly as obvious. He begins a relationship by having plenty of time for you and catering to your every whim and wish. He brings you flowers, buys you jewelry, and never shows up at the door without a bottle of wine or some other nicety. For all practical purposes, he's the perfect gentleman and, of course, your dream come true.

Once the relationship get comfortable, though, watch out! Your agenda is never quite as important as his. He insists that you leave work to come home and clean the house because he decided to throw a spur-of-the-moment party. He insists that you cancel your business trip because he wants you to help him with that project he's finally gotten around to. And when you balk, he quickly points out that he owns you. After all, he bought you all those nice things—and you definitely owe him something for that!

The Catch-22er

This Frog is suave, charming, and debonair. He courts you, praises you, and even helps you with your problems.

And unlike the Big Cheese, he'd never dream of assuming that his agenda is more important than yours. In fact, he not only encourages you to reach for your dreams, but outlines a surefire plan for grabbing them. Then he points out that you need to act quickly or they'll slip right through your fingers. You can't believe your good luck, and you wonder how you ever lived without him.

Once you finally decide to put his plan in place, though, the trouble begins. You discover that he really didn't want you to reach for your dreams at all. He only showed you the options so you'd realize that he was the only thing you needed for a full life. So you agree and tell him that he's right. That doesn't fix anything, though. Now you're a loser, a quitter, and someone who doesn't have the gumption it takes to be a success.

The Promiser

As with most of the other Frogs on this list, this ribbiter really knows how to court a lady. Gifts flow freely and flowers arrive at the door. In fact, he's even apt to hide fabulous little presents for you in unexpected places: the kitchen cabinets, the linen closet, or even your lingerie drawer. But that's not all. Loyal and chivalrous, he'll defend your honor to the death if necessary. Tossing you aside for another woman would never cross his mind. For all practical purposes, he's a knight in shining armor—the same knight you dreamt of for so long but didn't think existed.

The trouble only begins when it's time to ride off on the white horse. He asks you what you'd like to do or where you'd like to go. The sky's the limit, he says. Nothing is unattainable. (You, after all, hold the keys to his heart, and your happiness is all that matters to him.) You make a decision and apply for vacation time at work. He marks the calendar and goes about the business of making your fondest wish come true. Of course, none of it ever happens. He always backs out, and it's always at the last minute. He's too tired, too sick, or too broke. He doesn't like crowds. Your wishes, no matter what he said before, are simply unreasonable. That being the case, you'll spend your life doing what he wants to do—or sitting in front of the television rubbing his feet!

The Royal Pain

This Frog is usually the easiest to spot, for he is the Lord of the Manor, and everyone else is simply one of his subjects. The reason that we don't shun him immediately, though, is because—like the Victim—he makes us feel necessary. It starts out innocently enough. He wants a cup of coffee, a glass of tea, or maybe even dinner served to him in the living room. There's nothing wrong with that; we all like to be pampered once in a while.

The Royal Pain, however, never willingly helps with anything. He doesn't help with the cooking. He doesn't help with the cleaning. He doesn't help with the laundry. If he has to lift one finger to help with anything around the house, all hell breaks loose. He rants and raves that his every wish, whim, and need are solely your responsibility; all he should have to do is go to work and bring home a paycheck. Don't even bother to point out that he lives there, too, and that most of the mess lying around actually belongs to him. If he has to put away one thing, you'll hear about it for the rest of your life. Before it's said and done, you'll find yourself tending to everything and walking on eggshells to avoid the hassle. It's just so much easier than the alternative.

Soggy Ground:
Relationships Where Frogs Thrive

Even with this list in hand, you may have some trouble refusing these Frogs. Why? Frogs are, without a doubt, the most charming critters on the face of the Earth. Even though we usually don't realize it, charm is the first order of business when it comes to relationship chemistry. Without it, the heart simply isn't interested—and neither are we.

The best thing we can do for ourselves is avoid creating an environment conducive to amphibious comfort levels, an environment where Frogs can grow, thrive, and easily hop into our laps, and an environment created by such personal neediness that we fall into one of the categories that follow.

The Other Lover

When I played this role, I didn't think it was such a bad thing. After all, I didn't mind having lots of time on my hands, and I had friends to share in the festivities of my birthday and holidays. I talked myself into believing that this sort of relationship was absolutely perfect for me. I argued that I needed my space, the time to do what I wanted, and the freedom to act on my every whim. I believed that I couldn't get any of that in a "normal" relationship. Besides, my bills were getting paid and I never had to worry about washing someone else's dirty socks or underwear. I didn't see anything wrong with that—at least, not at first.

The problem occurred when reality set in and I finally took a good look at the situation. I discovered that my "partner" wasn't a partner at all. Everything was fine as long as he was getting exactly what he wanted. He truly didn't care about my opinions and couldn't be bothered with my needs. More to the point, everything he'd told me about his "other relationship" was not only a lie, but a lie so well-constructed and continuous that it could have filled the Grand Canyon. By that time, it was too late: I'd not only lost myself and my financial freedom, but I'd lost my heart as well.

The Wait Staff

Because the female human thrives on feeling necessary, even the most intelligent women manage to slip into this role from time to time. I've been there myself. That's because it all starts out as a simple act of kindness, an act so removed from anything harmful that we just don't see it coming. Make no mistake, though: It's just as damaging as playing the Other Lover—or a game of Russian roulette with your heart.

In my case, it began with getting my partner a glass of iced tea. It wouldn't have been a big deal except that I was folding clothes in the bedroom, and he was already in the kitchen— not six steps from the refrigerator door. I stopped what I was doing immediately, raced down the hall, and handed him a glass. It never occurred to me—at least, not at that point— that anything was even remotely out of kilter. How could it be? It was, for all practical purposes, a simple act of kindness.

What I didn't realize at the time was that I had just set a precedent for the next 16 years. I found myself waiting on him hand and foot. As soon as I'd sit down to dinner, the requests would begin. Of course, we never ate together. We couldn't. By the time I finally grabbed my seat, he was already done and calling for coffee from the living room.

Never once in all that time did I see a rented movie in its entirety. I was always too busy fixing snacks or getting drinks.

Never once did I enjoy the luxury of a nap on a lazy Saturday afternoon. I was always too busy locating some obscure tool for one of his projects. Never once was I able to enjoy one single, solitary uninterrupted conversation with a friend—at least, not when he was home. I was way too busy filling his every need, and doing it all in three- to five-minute intervals. But that wasn't the worst of it. One day I even found myself mopping up one of his messes the day after I'd had major surgery and discovered, to my horror, that he was annoyed because I hadn't done it sooner. In fact, life would have been much easier if I really had been a waitress; at least I'd have gotten tips and downtime!

The Doormat

This is another role that's easy to fall into, especially if you subscribe to the same life philosophy that I do. Simply put, it's this: If it won't matter in five years, why waste the energy? Practiced as it's meant to be, it's a very good philosophy. Just like everything else in life, though, it can be stretched to the max and run out of control. Such was the case with me.

It started out simply enough. It was merely a decision not to become embroiled in the fight of the century with my then-partner. After all, I reasoned, over a span of five years, I probably wouldn't even remember what had actually caused the ruckus. With that in mind, I thought out every word before I spoke, voiced my opinions in a very calm manner, and was extremely careful not to say anything I might regret later. When it became apparent that we were at an impasse and I was much too tired to continue, I finally uttered the simple words that I knew would bring the ordeal to an end: I'm sorry.

It was the biggest mistake of my life. My partner not only missed the point, but he viewed my kindness as a show of personal weakness. After that, no matter what happened in our lives, it all became totally and irrevocably my fault. That wasn't the worst of it, though. Any respect he'd had for me flew right out the window. Gradually, I became viewed as nothing more than the secretary, babysitter, maid, or whatever else struck his fancy on any given day. For all practical purposes, I was his personal doormat.

So why didn't I get out—or at least stop the insanity? Because it wasn't as easy as it sounds. Once all respect was gone, I didn't feel that I deserved any better. And that being the case, it was all I could do to put one foot in front of the other. Simple existence became a vicious cycle, one that I hope you'll never have to experience.

The Fairy Godperson

Everybody I know wishes he or she could wave a magic wand and make everything right with the world. Of course, no one can really do that. There are those of us, however, who do have a real knack for fixing things, turning situations around to our benefit, and pulling the proverbial rabbit out of the hat. Such was the case with me.

It started with the need to please and be appreciated. Something would go wrong—an error on the phone bill or bank statement, a credit card overcharge, or a problem with a hotel reservation—and I'd fix it. It wasn't a big deal, and the show of appreciation that followed was certainly worth the effort. Life was good. I was happy. After a while, I truly thought there was nothing that I couldn't handle.

Of course, I never realized that I was setting myself up. Once my "magic" became apparent, the problems grew by leaps and bounds. No matter how irresponsible the action, my partner just assumed I'd fix it. He went about his day doing exactly as he pleased, without one thought of retribution. He knew I'd handle it. He went on a shopping spree (a car, an ATV, and a boat) and left me to figure out how to pay for it. That was just the beginning.

I finally realized my limitations and announced that we couldn't go on like that. He announced that he had no intention of changing his lifestyle. What's more, he informed me that it was my job to handle whatever was thrown my way— that I *could* do it, that I'd *always* done it, and that I'd *continue* to do it. After all, his wish was my command.

As laughable as that sounds now, it was *anything* but funny at the time. I stayed awake at night from worry. I figured and calculated. I even went as far as to spend entire royalty checks trying to get us out of debt. It didn't help. In the final analysis, there was nothing for me to do but leave him, file bankruptcy, and start all over again. All of it could have been avoided if I hadn't been so needy at the onset.

Squashing the Frog

This advice is all well and fine, but what if you're already plagued with one of these Frogs? Even worse, what if you're firmly ensconced in soggy ground? One solution is to run faster and harder and longer than you've ever run before. Unfortunately, it's not always that easy. For one thing, Frogs seem to have radar when it comes to this sort of thing. Once they locate you again, they always seem to be able to ribbit their way back into your life.

There is a better solution: Completely eradicate everything from your life that Frogs find appealing and comforting.

Start by learning to say no. It's a simple word, it's easy to understand, and once you incorporate it into your vocabulary, it isn't that hard to say.

Of course, there's more to squashing Frogs than learning to spout one little word. If getting rid of them were that easy, they wouldn't be such a problem. In fact, we would never be plagued with them at all. The truth is that relieving ourselves of these critters takes exceptional strength and courage. We have to be rough, tough, and willing to go the distance. We have to be willing to let go of the familiar and embrace the unknown. Further, we have to know—deep down in our hearts—that we deserve better than they're ever going to be willing to give us. Because our hearts and minds don't always work well together, these concepts can be very difficult to accept.

That being the case, begin the eradication process by performing the ritual outlined in the following section. It will not only give you the strength to follow through, but it can be performed on any day at any time, regardless of the phase of the moon.

Frog-Eradication Ritual

Materials list:
    2 small pieces of black onyx
    1 black feather
    1 white candle

Begin by lighting the candle. Visualize its light and warmth growing until it totally envelops you. Then visualize yourself, your Frog, and the cosmic cords that connect you. These always connect the torso

but are usually located in the abdominal regions. Pick
up the feather and cut the cords one by one, saying
with each:

> I cut this cord that binds we two
> I cut it firmly through and through
> We feel no loss—there is no pain
> We feel relieved and whole again

When all the cords are severed, pick up the pieces
of black onyx. Hold them to your third eye (the spot
between your eyebrows) and visualize them glowing
with power. Say:

> Stone of separation—stone of will and
>   power
> Bring space between the two of us and
>   start this very hour
> Soak up remorse, absorb all hurt, and
>   lend me now your strength
> Allow me to remove myself regardless
>   of the length
> Of time that we have been together, for
>   the damage that we do
> To each other must stop now so life can
>   start anew
> Give me peace and courage and the
>   strength to separate
> And bring a smile unto our lips as I walk
>   out the gate

Place the stones before the candle and leave them
there until the flame extinguishes itself. Then carry
one stone with you and give the other to your partner.
Separation will come peacefully within two weeks.

Mend-a-Broken-Heart Spell

Even when we know we've done the right thing, ending a relationship can be painful. That's because no matter how damaging a relationship is (or how well we understand that), the heart rarely accepts any decision made by the mind. Instead, it screams, yells, and whimpers in pain. And when we hold fast to what we know to be good for us, the heart resorts to more drastic measures. Before it's said and done, the heart relieves us of all common sense—and we find ourselves in second-guess mode. Suddenly, we begin to believe that which was so damaging (the very stuff that nearly did us in) wasn't so bad after all. In fact, we often find ourselves trying to reopen a door that should have been locked and barred long ago.

This doesn't have to happen to you. This spell is designed not only to ease the pain but also to silence all that incessant nonsense spouted by your heart.

Materials list:
1 black candle
1 white candle
1 small piece of amethyst
1 small piece of rose quartz
Lemon oil (lemon furniture polish will
do in a pinch)
Floral oil of your choice

On the day before the new moon, gather together the black candle, amethyst, and lemon oil. Inscribe the source of the heart's misery on the candle. A lengthy description isn't necessary; in fact, because it's best to keep it simple, you may just want to inscribe a heart with a jagged line drawn down the middle. Anoint the candle by first rubbing a few drops of the oil between your palms. Then grasp the candle firmly at the center with both hands. Working outward toward the ends, rub the oil around the circumference of the candle and on both ends. After the candle is anointed, put it aside.

Hold the stone to your third eye and concentrate on all the pain caused by the relationship. Then release the misery and will it to flow into the stone. Once you're absolutely certain that every shred of pain is gone, place the stone in front of the candle, light the wick, and say:

> To you, black candle, I lend light
> Bring immediate change with power and
>   might:
> Change of heart and change of pain
> Change my loss into my gain
> Within this stone all hurt be trapped
> So it's source cannot be tapped
> Or harm another on its way
> As I will, do what I say

Let the candle burn completely down, then take the stone outside and throw it with all the strength you can muster. Bury any leftover wax as far away from your property as possible.

On the next day (the day of the new moon) inscribe the white candle with the words *hope, joy,* and *laughter,* and anoint it with a floral-scented oil that appeals to you. (Lotus, magnolia, wisteria, and jasmine are all good choices.) Hold the rose quartz to your third eye and visualize yourself living a happy life. See yourself laughing, surrounded by friends, and positively enveloped in the warmth of possibility and fresh opportunity. Then place the stone in front of the candle, light the wick, and say:

> Upon you, candle of purest white
> I bestow the gift of light
> And with that burning, dancing flame
> I command that you reclaim
> Joy and opportunity
> Personal community
> Laughter, happiness, and fun
> And once your gathering is done
> Bring it quickly back to me
> As I will, so mote it be

Let the candle burn down completely, then carry the stone with you. Bury any leftover wax on your property or in one of your houseplants.

After the Rituals

You've squashed the Frog and performed the rituals. That being the case, you're forever free of life's proverbial ribbiters, right? Well, not exactly. Once you've escaped their clutches and healed any residual pain you still have work to do. Simply put, you need to learn something from your mistakes and do everything in your power not to repeat them. Otherwise, all the magic in the world isn't going to help. You will just keep being inundated with Frogs until you're green in the face. If your choices have brought only Frogs to date, you may need some help in breaking the pattern. That's where the three little words that follow come in. They're the same words that your parents taught you to use when crossing the street. Study them carefully and use them well; they will help to put you back on solid ground—a place where Frogs won't dare to hop.

Stop. Someone once told me not to date anyone I wouldn't want to marry. Although the statement seemed utterly ridiculous at the onset, I finally found its sense. Simply put, it means that time spent getting to know someone on a casual level is imperative before joining him or her in an intimate relationship. For this reason, exercise some caution when it comes to finding a suitable mate. Ask lots of questions. Evaluate the answers. Finally, ask for a phone number. If this request is refused for any reason, you can nearly count on the fact that the person in question is already taken and definitely not worth your trouble.

Look. Because actions speak louder than words, it pays to take note of how a potential love interest interacts with others. Why? Because his or her behavior is a direct reflection of how you will be treated in the future. If you're pleased with what you see, then check out the sort of people the person counts as friends. Because like usually attracts like, this will give you some insight into the real person hiding beneath the surface, and that's something you'll want to see before you go any further.

Listen. My mother used to say that anyone who talked as much as my ex-husband did couldn't possibly be telling the truth all of the time. She was right. Understand that not everyone tells the truth. If a potential mate says something that doesn't sound right to you, take it upon yourself to investigate. Although this may sound a bit dishonest at first, nothing could be further from the truth. Just remember that it's *your* heart on the line and the burden of proof is yours.

Frog Repellant Bath

Because froggy habits are hard to break, you may need more than the just-mentioned Stop, Look, Listen list to put you on the right road. In that case, try the Frog repellant bath below. Used with the list, it's the best way I know to keep future Frogs from invading your life.

Materials list:

1 T. dried basil
1 T. dried rosemary
3 drops patchouli oil
1 small glass vial with screw-on cap
Paper coffee filter
Wooden spoon
Rubber band
Automatic-drip coffeemaker

Begin by running a pot of water through your automatic-drip coffeemaker. Then place one table-spoon each of dried basil and dried rosemary in the center of a paper coffee filter. Secure the edges with a rubber band to form a bundle, toss it into the pot of hot water, and let it steep for 20 minutes. Add three drops of patchouli oil and, stirring the mixture coun-terclockwise with a wooden spoon, chant:

Herbs mix and oil meld
With this solution; be now spelled
To keep all Frogs away from me
As I will, so mote it be

Pour a tablespoon of the infusion into a small glass vial with a screw-on lid, cap tightly, and set aside. Pour the rest of the solution into your bath water. Immerse yourself completely in the water nine times and let your body dry naturally. Rub one drop of the bottled mixture into each temple every day (until you run out) and chant:

Of all Frogs, my path be free
As I will, so mote it be

Conjuring Princes

Once you've gotten rid of the Frogs, it's time to conjure your Prince or Princess. Anyone can do it. It simply isn't that hard. The difficulty comes in conjuring the one who's exactly right for you, because no matter how you slice it, one person's royalty could very well be another person's Frog. It pays to spend some time thinking long and hard about what sort of mate really appeals to you.

Royal Recipes

Start by making a list of all the outer qualities that appeal to you. It's very important to be specific here. If having plenty of money trips your trigger, write it down. If a particular body type makes you drool, add that, too. If you're only attracted to folks with red hair and green eyes, be sure it makes the list. This is no time to feel guilty about what you want. You are, after all, drawing up a blueprint for your very own mate. And no one knows your needs better than you do.

Next, give some serious thought to personality and the characteristics that should comprise the inner Prince or Princess. This is *not* something to rush through, for these are the very things that will keep your relationship going long after good looks and hot sex go by the wayside. Start this list with the following items. They comprise the most basic qualities that every perfect mate should have, and leaving them out is just asking for trouble.

- ଔ Charm.
- ଔ Consideration for others.
- ଔ Good communications skills.
- ଔ Good listening skills.
- ଔ Good lover.
- ଔ Good sense of humor.
- ଔ Helpfulness.
- ଔ Honesty.
- ଔ Kindness.
- ଔ Loving nature.
- ଔ Patience.
- ଔ Understanding.
- ଔ Unmarried.

Once you've gotten these down, add anything else that would make someone your perfect mate. For example, if fidelity is important to you, leaving it out could spell travesty. The same goes for a gentle touch. This is no time to leave things to chance. What you write on this list is precisely what will manifest, so it pays to take your time and get it right.

You may not be able to put the list together in one sitting. In fact, it may take several days to several weeks to get this all down. Just put it in perspective and remember that this time you're not designing some cute and pleasant fly-by-night diversion. You are building your perfect mate, someone with whom you intend to spend the rest of your life. And that's just too important to hurry through.

The Soul Mate Fallacy

Somewhere along the line, we've all gotten the idea that conjuring the perfect love has something to do with finding our soul mate—and that Prince Charming or Princess Perfect absolutely, positively, beyond the shadow of a doubt must be that person. Otherwise, we'll never be truly happy. We'll never be truly satisfied. Even worse, we'll spend the rest of our lives searching for that other half that truly makes us whole.

It sounds good. It sounds logical. It even fuels the inner core, for there's nothing more romantic than the thought of another being whose soul is intertwined with ours for all eternity. Unfortunately, it's also the biggest load of crap that society ever expected us to swallow.

It's not that soul mates don't exist. (They do.) It's not that each of us don't have at least one. (Most of us have several.) It's just that finding that person—and connecting with him or her—doesn't necessarily constitute finding the love of a lifetime. It just doesn't work that way. Here's why: When we love and trust someone, we actually give a piece of ourselves away. That piece is a part of our personal energy field or aura. Simply put, it's a part of the soul. It's not something that we mean to do. It's automatic and involuntary. It's just a part of what happens during the love relationship. That being the case, it stands to reason that we can accumulate several soul mates during the course of one lifetime (and hundreds during the course of reincarnative living). This makes the chances of having only one soul mate very slim indeed.

Just for the sake of argument, though, let's say that you really are the one in a million who possesses only one soul mate. How do you know if that person really and truly loved you through eternity? How do you know if your love was even reciprocated? More to the point, how do you know that your soul mate wasn't a Frog? You don't, and you probably never will.

A soul mate is nothing more than a person with whom you have unfinished karmic business. It's only someone with whom a score must be settled. That score could be anything from a communications problem to a simple misunderstanding, but it could also be a slimy affair that nearly wrenched the heart right out of your chest. Because you're reading this book, that's obviously a place you don't want to go.

For this reason, please resist any urges to add the words *soul mate* to your list. Doing so is just asking for trouble. If the perfect love you conjure really is a soul mate, so be it. But if that's not the case, omitting this one little detail could definitely raise the odds for romantic perfection—and that's something that wouldn't be possible if you unwittingly opened the door and invited yet one more Frog to hop into your life.

Perfecting the Design

Once your list is in order, it's time to perfect the design. This means taking a few moments to think about the following. Although we certainly like to imagine the ideal mate as being perfect in every way, such is not the case. Even the most perfect people are human; we all come with flaws. It's simply a matter of knowing which flaws you can live with and which ones you can't. For this reason, list the things that really annoy you—anything from spitting in the toilet to smacking chewing gum—on a separate sheet of paper. Then transform each annoyance into a positive quality and add it to your design list. (A sample list follows as an example.)

Annoyance	Positive Quality
Leaves toilet seat up	Puts the toilet down
Is untidy	Puts things away
Has a bad temper	Is calm, even in anger
Is careless with money	Is thrifty
Is self-centered	Is caring
Smacks gum	Chews gum discreetly

One More Thing...

Although we've already discussed how important it is to be specific in your listings, I can't stress it enough. Here's why: A friend of mine once drew up such a list, and even though she took her time and worked with specifics I'd never have even considered (such as zodiac sign and sample compatibility charts) she got something other than expected. It wasn't that things didn't work; they did. Magic not only materialized precisely to her specifications, but everything was right

on target. The only problem was that her Prince Charming—
that wonderful creature who would adore her forever—didn't
manifest in the form of a man at all. He came in the form of a
dog.

Of course, it never occurred to either one of us that this
could happen. It probably wouldn't occur to you either. So
be warned: Never leave this sort of thing to chance. Remember that the universe doesn't think. It's a black-and-white
sort of entity that lives and breathes and works within distinct separations—separations in which gray areas simply
don't exist.

In light of that, I not only urge you to add "human being" to your list, but to list gender as well. You may even
want to take things a step further and list sexual preference;
in fact, I'd suggest it strongly. Why? Because I can't think of
anything more emotionally, mentally, or magically frustrating
than setting yourself up to fall in love with someone who will
never—regardless of how firmly your hearts are connected—
freely enter into a romantic relationship with you. It's just
setting yourself up for trouble. And that's a place you don't
want to go.

For this reason, make the applicable additions and go
through your list with a fine-toothed comb to check any other
missing items. When the list meets your needs, rewrite it
neatly in red ink on white paper. Fold the list into thirds,
then into thirds again. You're now ready to actively begin
the conjuring process.

Ritual Preparations

I usually recommend that folks alter spells and rituals to
reflect personal taste and style. This particular rite, however, is
the exception to the rule. That's because when it's followed to

the letter, it comprises the most powerful magic I've ever encountered. And because it's not broken, there's just no reason to fix it!

C3 **Check your calendar.** To ensure success, work this
spell on a Friday. The reason for this is simple:
Friday is ruled by Venus, the planet of love, and
spells involving love and romance are most effective when performed under that influence. If
you want additional insurance, look for a Friday
when the moon is waxing or growing larger in the
sky. Even better, schedule the spell for a Friday
during a full moon.

C3 **Find a quiet place to work.** Most folks immediately head for the bedroom, but I've found this
spell to be much more effective when performed
in the kitchen. The reasons are multifaceted.
Because the kitchen is the heart of the home and
the place from which our physical nourishment
flows, it speaks to us on a mundane level. The
aromas we associate with that area (baking bread,
simmering stew, and so forth) bring strong mental and emotional messages that make us feel
loved. The use of this room speaks to all three
levels of our being—the conscious, the subcon-
scious, and the unconscious—simultaneously, and
such communication truly makes us one with the
effort. Most important, though, we want life with
Prince Charming to be a well-rounded, happy, and
loving experience. The best way to accomplish that
is to connect him not only with your heart, but
also with the heart of the home. Because it sym-
bolizes the matrix from which home life stems, it
makes living happily ever after a given.

❧ **Gather your materials.** For this spell, you'll need a white candle, a pink candle, and a red candle. The size of the candles makes no difference here. Pillars, tapers, and votives work equally well. Even birthday candles will do. You'll also need a metal cookie sheet, a box of table salt, and the "blueprint" list you created previously in this chapter.

The Ritual

When conjuring day arrives, begin by placing the cookie sheet lengthwise on the countertop. Place the white candle at the center point of the left-hand edge of the pan. Working across in a horizontal fashion, place the pink candle next to the white and the red candle next to the pink. Using the box of salt, draw a heart at the center point of the right-hand edge of the pan. Then use the salt to draw an arrow from the red candle through the heart, making sure that the arrow point intersects the center of the heart.

Take a few deep breaths and relax. Then light the white candle while thinking about the cosmos working with you to make your perfect mate materialize. Visualize this person in every detail *except* for facial features. (This is very important, because you don't want this spell to work on someone who isn't perfectly suited to you. If you have difficulty with this, either visualize the person from the rear or with the head turned in such a way that facial features aren't visible.)

Light the pink candle. Visualize yourself in the process of a perfect romance with the person. (Again, be sure not to add a face!) Make it playful and fun but also deep and meaningful. Make it everything that true love and romance are to you.

Light the red candle. Visualize yourselves caught up in the sheer ecstasy of hot, passionate lovemaking. Make it soft and gentle. Make it wild and lustful. Make it whatever you like. Just remember to avoid facial features at all costs.

Place the folded list inside the salt heart and visualize your potential mate having all the characteristics described on the list. Visualize that person as being everything you desire and more. Let the candles burn all the way down.

When the candles burn out, set the list on fire and place it back in the heart of salt. As the list burns to ash, say:

> My Prince/Princess you are—my Prince/
>   Princess you'll be
> As paper burns, I conjure thee
> Manifest and breathe new life
> Find me quickly without strife
> Hurry, hurry unto me
> As I will, so mote it be

When the ashes cool, use a knife to loosen any remaining candle wax. Bury all of the spell ingredients (salt, ashes, and wax) outside. If that's not possible, bury them in a potted plant. It works just as well (and it won't harm the plant).

After the Ritual

Once you've completed the ritual, just kick back and re-lax. Don't worry that your love won't arrive. (It will happen.) There's no need for concerns that you screwed something up. (You didn't.) Above all, don't even consider the possi-bility that the ritual won't work. (It not only *will,* but the magic's already begun.) Because of the magnitude of what you're demanding of the cosmos, though—you are, after all, expecting a worldwide search for your perfect mate—results may take a little time. In fact, it could take several months. That being the case, there's just no need to be antsy.

If you feel that you *must* do something to hurry things alongand after about three weeks, if you're anything like the rest of the population, you will—a gentle nudge to the uni-verse is perfectly fine. Here's where love attractants come in. These great little tools not only remind the universe to get with the program, but they open your heart to endless roman-tic possibility. The worst-case scenario is that you'll be the most sought-after date since the Cinderella/Prince Charming regime. The best-case scenario, though, is that your love will come riding in with such speed and focus that you'll be swept right off your feet. Either way, it's great stuff.

There are more ways to attract love than you can shake a stick at, so it's impossible to list them all in this book. For that reason, I've only listed a few of my very favorites. Use them alone or in combination. Rework them to suit your personal lifestyle and preference. Or just use them as a guideline to create your very own attraction method, something designed especially to speed the manifestation of your heart's desire. (For best results, construct these attractants on a Friday dur-ing new to full moon.)

ଓଃ **Wear fragrance.** Don't wear just any fragrance, though. Wear something especially created to attract your mate. Start with one ounce of grape seed or jojoba oil, then blend in a few drops of love-attracting essential oils. The unisex recipes that follow will get you started, but don't be afraid to experiment a little. In fact, you may want to whip up your own recipe using alternative oils. (For ideas, check the herbs listed in Appendix A.)

Hearts and Flowers Attractant

4 drops rosewood or jasmine oil
1 drop patchouli oil
1 drop myrrh oil

Passionate Love Attractant

4 drops vanilla oil
1 drop clove oil
1 drop rosewood oil

As you blend the oils, say:

> Prince/Princess of mine—love to be
> I await you! Come to me!

Wear the perfume every day, dabbing a bit behind your ears, on the nape of your neck, in the bends of your elbows, and behind your knees. Alternatively, add six drops of the oil to a cup of salt and add a tablespoon or two to your daily bath. You'll be amazed at the response!

ଓଃ **Scent the air around you.** Although this can be handled in several different ways, the easiest is to dab a bit of your personal oil on the light bulbs in your home. If you prefer a stovetop potpourri or something more visually aesthetic, try this recipe. It definitely sends out love signals and works equally well in baskets or pots.

Heartstrings Potpourri

2 c. dried rose petals or buds
1/2 c. dried apple peel or slices
1/4 c. dried lavender
6 cinnamon sticks
6 T. whole cloves
1 T. allspice
1 tsp. vanilla oil

Mix well, saying the chant from the love attractants, then place in potpourri baskets. Alternatively, add a tablespoon or two to a pot of water and allow it to simmer on the stove. (If you're using the stovetop method, remember to check water levels occasionally.)

⚛ **Enchant a clear quartz crystal.** Once you've conjured Prince Charming or Princess Perfect, you may feel the need to have a radar device of sorts—something, if you will, to help your perfect mate track you down. In this case, nothing works better than a clear quartz crystal. Just hold the stone in your dominant hand and concentrate on your true love finding you. Once the stone begins to pulse—and it will—chant:

> I command you, clear quartz stone—
> No matter where I go or roam—
> To bring my true love straight to me
> As I will, so mote it be

Carry the stone with you constantly.

⚛ **Construct and wear a love-attracting charm.** Special note to men: There's no need to bother with the ribbons when making this charm. Just sew the heart, stuff it with the ingredients listed, and carry it in your pocket. (Incidentally, guys, this is a great ice-breaker. Simply ask a lady if she'd like to see your love charm, and pull it out of your pocket. Once her laughter dies down, the conversation is sure to flow!)

Materials list:

- 2 4-inch squares of red, pink, or rose-colored fabric (taffeta, satin, and velveteen are all good choices)
- 3-1/2 yds. ¼-inch ribbon in a shade that matches the fabric
- 2 apple seeds
- 2 rose petals
- 1 tiny magnet or a lodestone with metal filings
- 1 strand of your hair
- 1 small rose quartz
- 1 pinch cinnamon
- Vanilla oil (or your personal oil)
- Small heart charm, venice lace, etc. (optional)
- Needle, thread, pins, pencil, and scissors

Cut the ribbon into six equal sections and set aside. Place the two squares of fabric one on top of the other with the right sides together, then fold them in half. Using the pencil, draw a half heart along the fold line and carefully cut along the lines with sharp scissors. Unfold the heart.

Gather the ribbons into groups of three and align the ends of one group, placing them one on top of the other. Place the ends on top of the heart even with the upper inverted point. Secure with pins. Repeat the process with the other group.

Starting at the bottom point and using a ¼-inch seam allowance, stitch the hearts together. Stop stitching about a half inch from the bottom point, knot the thread, and turn the heart inside out.

Add the seeds, petals, magnet, hair, stone, and cinnamon while using the preceding love-attractant chant, then stitch the opening closed. Braid the ribbons, tying with knots, to secure the ends. Decorate the heart with lace or charms if desired, then wear the heart around your neck as a choker. It can also be worn as an anklet if that's more your style.

Are you ready?

So, you've conjured the perfect mate. The universe is searching. By the time you read this, it's safe to say that you've not only made a personal love charm, but are holding it so tight that it may have to be surgically removed. Chances are, though, you haven't given any thought to how you'll react when love—that awesome wonder you've been working so hard to find—appears from nowhere and knocks on your door. Will you know it's the real thing? Will you slam the door in fear of it being just one more Frog? Or will you simply saunter down the garden path completely oblivious to its arrival?

These are serious considerations, especially if you've been hurt before. Although it's only human nature to be gun-shy after a bad experience, this simply will not do if you're expecting to find the love of a lifetime. You have to be open, willing to take a chance, and, of course, willing to embrace whatever comes your way. Otherwise, it won't matter how hard love knocks. Nothing—not even something as powerful as true love—can enter a door that's been locked and barred.

The key here is twofold. First, you have to keep the proverbial door open. Second, and just as important, you must chase away any fear fragments left behind by previous relationships. Because that's easier said than done, I've provided some assistance in the form of a ritual. The success of the ritual does not depend upon proper moon phase or day of the week, so it may be performed at any time. Once you've performed it, though, understand that there's no going back. You'll be ready, willing, and able to accept the love that comes your way. That life of solitude you now live will certainly be a thing of the past!

The Love-Preparedness Ritual

Materials list:

- 1 purple candle
- 1 pink candle
- 1 white candle
- 1 stick dragon's blood incense or ¼ tsp. resin
- 1 charcoal block (unnecessary if you use stick incense)
- Pencil

Begin by lighting the charcoal block and sprinkling some dragon's blood incense or resin on top. Using the pencil, carve a small key on the purple candle. (This doesn't have to be a perfect rendition. It's only important that you know what it is.) Light the candle and visualize yourself being open to the love that awaits you. Once the image is clear, appeal to the goddesses of locks and doors by chanting:

> Carne and Syn of Locks and Doors
> Open my heart as never before
> Leave me wide open for what shall arrive:
> That wondrous love for which I now
>   strive

Carve two intersecting circles on the pink candle to symbolize a hug. Visualize yourself embracing the love that is coming, and then appeal to Aphrodite by chanting:

> Great Aphrodite, please show me the way
> To embrace what is coming—and start
>   now, today
> To prepare for the love that is rushing
>   toward me
> To accept it and hold it as what it
>   should be

Carve a heart with an arrow through it on the white candle. Visualize all previous hurt being erased by pure white light. Then appeal to Eros, saying:

> And masterful Eros, I ask Your help,
>   too
> That I know in a heartbeat that such
>   love is true
> By the strength of your arrow, and
>   straightforward shot
> Erase any thoughts of the loves that
>   were not

Finally, see yourself completely prepared for the love that you've conjured. Appeal to all four deities by chanting:

I ask that You four work together as One
Until all the tasks I've requested are
    done
And once I'm prepared and all is
    achieved
With my fondest blessings, You may all
    take Your leave

Once the candles burn completely down, bury any leftover wax in the ground.

Before We Go Any Further...

By now, you should be absolutely inundated with potential mates vying for your attention. At any rate, you should be having a really good time. That being the case, it's time for a little warning: Simply put, the system that follows in the rest of this book is, indeed, the most potent love magic you'll ever encounter. Use it with caution. Use it with care. And for Goddess's sake, make absolutely, positively certain that the person you use it on is, beyond the shadow of a doubt, your Prince Charming or Princess Perfect. Otherwise, you'll definitely have more on your hands than you bargained for. How do I know? Because it happened to me.

Sadly enough, I never realized that something so seemingly unmagical could pack such a wallop. In fact, it seemed too easy to work. I just had to give it a whirl to prove that it wouldn't. I was wrong. Not only did it work, but it worked thoroughly and immediately. But that wasn't the worst of it: The results were so long-lasting that nothing seemed to slow it down, not magic, not rudeness, and not even my brand-new wedding ring.

This man tried everything in his power to get me back. There were phone calls, cards, and letters. When those were unsuccessful, he sent flowers—not just a vase or two, mind you, but nearly every blossom in the shop. He finally became so obsessed that he even feigned a life-threatening illness. He just couldn't understand why I wouldn't leave my husband to come tend to him. That, of course, was the last straw. I called the police, who, together with a psychiatrist, treated him to a nice little vacation. It was a horrible mess that lasted more than 16 years. To think that I could have avoided the whole thing by simply exercising a little caution!

Please don't misunderstand. The system that follows is perfectly safe when used with a lifetime commitment in mind. If you're not sure that the current Prince or Princess is your perfect mate, then that in itself is your answer. When your perfect mate arrives, you'll know beyond the shadow of a doubt that he or she is not just someone you could live with, but someone whom you can't live without. That's the time to put the following system in gear and drive it home, full-speed ahead.

Chapter Three

Dancing in Glass Slippers

So you've found the perfect mate, you're positively infatuated, and you're ready to ride away on the white horse. Not so fast. First you need to learn to communicate. Otherwise, all your trouble will be for naught. For even the most charming folks in the world can take on Froglike characteristics if they're misunderstood (or if they think they are).

Communicating can be likened to dancing in glass slippers. Why? Because even though we've been expressing ourselves for years and think we know how, truly effective communication can be a bit tricky. All it takes is one false step, and idea exchanges and message transmissions not only break, but also usually shatter beyond repair. Fortunately, there is a solution. We just have to learn which words the brain accepts freely and which ones it tosses aside.

Simply put, the human brain has difficulty when it comes to processing words in their negative forms. In fact, it rarely even bothers to process them at all. Think I'm kidding? How many times, for example, have you asked someone *not* to forget something only to discover that they have? What about the times that you've specifically requested that someone *not* do something and—even after you've outlined some very good reasons—found that your request fell on deaf ears? If you're anything like me, you probably can't even begin to remember all the instances, much less count them. The reason for this is that the brain absolutely refused to process the word *not* and the parties involved never even heard it. They simply went on about their business, did what they thought was right, and emerged completely bewildered at your obvious annoyance.

For this reason, take a good look at the sentence examples that follow. They provide perfect illustrations of what is said versus what is really processed.

Conversational examples

- ☙ "*Don't* forget to pick up the dry cleaning."
  (The brain hears: "Forget to pick up the dry cleaning.")

- ☙ "*Never* doubt my love for you."
  (The brain hears: "Doubt my love for you.")

- ☙ "You *can't* do that."
  (The brain hears: "You do that.")

- ☙ "That *won't* work."
  (The brain hears: "That works.")

- ☙ "I *neither* agree with you, *nor* support you in this."
  (The brain hears: "I agree with you and support you in this.")

This is no way to start a relationship, especially not one that you intended to stand the test of time. We need to learn to speak a different language—a language that the brain not only understands, but can process easily and perfectly every time.

This isn't as hard as it sounds. All we have to do is learn which words to eliminate from our vocabularies. The following list offers a good starting point.

- ☙ Don't.

- ☙ Can't.

- ☙ Won't.

- ☙ Never.

- ☙ Neither/nor.

- ☙ Forget/ignore.

If we handle our conversations without these words (see the examples that follow this paragraph) our communications run true to form, and our messages are crystal clear. The brain knows exactly what we want and expect. Thus we have a much better chance of getting what we need. This not only makes us happier people, but it increases the relationship success rate by 100 percent.

Conversational replacement examples

ᘓ "Please remember to pick up the dry cleaning."

ᘓ "Always know that I love you."

ᘓ "I'd feel better if you handled it this way."

ᘓ "Let's rethink this."

ᘓ "How about a compromise?"

Love Matches

Now that we've gotten the basics out of the way, the next step is to find out precisely what kind of person your Prince or Princess is. Although people come in all shapes, sizes, and colors, there are really only three categories when it comes to finding your love match: sound, sight, and emotion. A good way to illustrate this is to take any two people and put them in a set of like circumstances. Seldom, if ever, will they react identically (mentally, physically, or emotionally) in the same situation. Why? Because they are usually two distinctly different types of people. They each speak their own language. Because of this, determining your love's type is especially important. After all, if you don't learn how to speak in a language that he or she understands, you can't possibly expect to have any sort of effective or lasting relationship.

This may sound difficult, but it's not. All it takes is a keen eye and the ability to really listen to any words that roll off the tongue. That said, let's take an in-depth look at specific language types.

Lovers of Sound

These folks are usually the easiest to spot because they tend to prop their heads up with a hand, as if they were talking on the phone. They like the sounds of their own voices, simply love being called by name, and have a tendency to glance side to side instead moving their eyes straight up and down.

Another set of determining factors come from the sorts of pastimes they enjoy. Though they will watch television with another person, they much prefer listening to music. For this reason, their free time seldom involves spectator sports. You're more likely to find them at a concert, the opera, or a lecture series, or actively participating in some sort of theater performance.

The biggest clue that you're dealing with a lover of sound, however, come from the words with which they choose to communicate, so listen carefully to the casual remarks that flow off their tongues. You'll find that a good many of them have to do with sounds. Here are some of the most common:

❧ "Did you *hear* what I said?"

❧ "That *sounds* like fun!"

❧ "*Listen!*"

❧ "Can we *talk*?"

- ◌ৎ "*Tell* me what you think."

- ◌ৎ "That *noise* really grates on my nerves."

- ◌ৎ "*Speak* up."

- ◌ৎ "Can you lower the *volume*?"

- ◌ৎ "I'm not *deaf*."

- ◌ৎ "Are you *listening* to me?"

If your love frequently speaks in auditory terms and exhibits several of the other attributes described here, he or she is probably auditory. This means that you have an edge, because unlike the other two types, this person will always respond to the sound of your voice as well as to the language of sound.

Lovers of Sight

These people generally glance upward when talking or thinking—as if they're somehow trying to pull a pictorial memory from the recesses of their minds. They love to create art and have a fondness for drawing, painting, and anything else that involves color. They have an exceptional love for color and design and even as children often have a better sense of fashion than their parents. They like mirrors, are frequently fascinated by photographs, and sometimes will spend an incredible amount of time simply watching a spider spin a web or an army of ants at work. If these descriptions fit your love interest, pay attention to the phrases that pop up in his or her casual conversations.

- ◌ৎ "*Look*!"

- ◌ৎ "Do you *see* what I mean?"

ଓ "I don't like the *looks* of that!"

ଓ "I get the *picture* now!"

ଓ "It *appears* to be a good idea."

ଓ "Your *view* and mine don't mesh."

ଓ "I don't *see* it that way!"

ଓ "You can't *see* the forest for the trees."

ଓ "I was so angry that I *saw red*!"

ଓ "I think your *perception* is *flawed*."

If your love frequently speaks in visual terms, he or she is more than likely a lover of sight. Although these folks won't automatically respond to the sound of your voice, they do respond to the color combinations you wear, the sights you describe, your decorating ideas, and the food that you serve (provided that it's arranged artfully on the plate).

Lovers of Emotion

Getting a handle on these folks can prove a bit trickier than the other two, because the signals they transmit are usually more subtle than those connected to sound or sight types. However, they do tend to look away or down to one side when considering something that's been said, as if they are trying to recall the memory of a relevant feeling from deep within their hearts. They like fabric texture, tend to wear clothes that feel good against their skin, and are big supporters of double-doses of fabric softener when it comes to doing laundry. (You will never, for example, find a lover of emotion wearing unlined wool in any shape, form, or fashion!)

They are the touchers of the universe and often the first to offer a hug or kiss, or worry about a baby bird that's fallen from the nest. Occasionally, they also have an obsession with their bodies, and even the smallest paper cut can be a major catastrophe. Most often, though, these people are discovered by the process of eliminating the other two types. If you suspect your love might fall into this category, check your conversations for these phrases:

ᑲ "Do you *know* what I *mean*?"

ᑲ "This doesn't *feel* right!"

ᑲ "Get a *grip*!"

ᑲ "I'm not *comfortable* with this."

ᑲ "I *hate* it when that happens."

ᑲ "I *love* the way that tastes."

ᑲ "That *hurt* my feelings."

ᑲ "It makes me *feel warm* and *fuzzy* all over."

ᑲ "This requires a *gentle touch*."

If your love doesn't fit the sound or sight categories, displays most of the attributes just listed, and talks frequently in terms of touch or feeling, he or she is definitely a lover of emotion.

Sometimes a person will exhibit an attribute or two from each category. If that happens, don't fret! Just pick the category that best fits your love and know that you've made the right decision. Every person fits into one of the categories, and there is no such thing as a person who fits equally well into several.

Putting it All Together

Now that you've targeted your love, how do you use the information to develop your relationship? You simply learn to talk in terms that he or she understands, structure your conversation so that it appeals to the correct type of person, and communicate your needs in such a way that the brain can process the information.

Let's say, for example, that your love is a man of sight who likes to play video games, watch old movies, and participate in indoor activities that involve art, design, graphics, and color. You, on the other hand, just can't get enough of the wild outdoors. Can the two of you happily find common ground? More to the point, is it possible for him to not only share your interests, but also enjoy them? Absolutely! It's just a matter of how you approach the subject and you handle your delivery. A good illustration follows in this sample situation:

> You say, *"Look, darlin'! There's something outside that I really want to show you. It's beautiful!"*

Chances are your partner will comply just because you've spoken to him on his own terms. But what if he doesn't? What if your Prince of Sight says, instead, "Maybe after this movie is over. Have you seen the special effects on this thing? They're absolutely incredible!"

This is where things get creative. Your best bet is to appeal to the side of him that's still a child. Let him know that you were perfectly willing to share this lovely thing with him because he's a special part of your life and you adore him, but now that you've thought it through, you'd just as soon keep it to yourself. From now on, tell him, it will be your little secret, your special place. He'll be hooked before you can get out the door, because no "child" likes to have secrets kept from him. (If that doesn't work, try a nature video!)

Once you've gotten his attention, the next step is to find a way to keep it. Although simple outdoor beauty may thrill him at first, it's not a good idea to rely solely upon its magic. You need to find something else, something that will continue to interest him, entice him, and ultimately fascinate him. Otherwise, you'll wind up sitting at home watching old movies and playing video games until you're old and gray.

Don't fret! All you need is a bag of tools geared to his personality type. Good tool choices for the Lover of Sight include sketchpads, pencils, charcoal, pastels, or some other art form that appeals to him. If he's more the instant-gratification type, pack a camera and extra rolls of film. You get the idea.

Once you get to the woods, spend some time discovering his interests. Point out a few tracks; gear a conversation toward the animals who made them, their habits, and personalities. See where it goes. If that's a dead end, take him on a search for wild herbs. His interests might even lie in the tadpoles and minnows that play in the stream. Although it may take some time to figure out precisely what captivates him, one thing's for sure. You'll find something out there that catches his eye—and when you do, you'll know exactly which interest to cultivate and how to keep him happy on your turf.

Dressing for Love

The best formula for total enchantment has to do with comfort. People just don't fall in love unless they're totally comfortable with each other. Finding that comfort level in love dressings has nothing to do with lace-up corsets and garter belts. (They have their place, but we'll address that later!) It has to do with a familiar, relaxed atmosphere, the sort of atmosphere that breeds contentment.

I can almost see you scratching your head at this point, especially at that last word. That's because we've been conditioned to believe that contentment is *anything* but sexy. In fact, most of us are brought up to see contentment as dull and boring. We think it's the final step before falling into a relationship rut and the final straw that makes us look elsewhere for excitement. But it's just not so, especially when dealing with real love. Not only can we be comfortable *and* sexy, but we can manage to do it all at the same time. All we have to do is take a cue from our perfect mates and pay attention to what they're wearing when they're courting.

For example, not all Princes are the Ivy-league type. Those who are always dress accordingly. You'll never find them wearing a three-piece suit, for example, when escorting you to a ball game on the hottest day of the year. Instead, they'll be wearing shorts and a T-shirt. Jeans will work for a movie and dinner. An outing to the park might just call for their favorite sweats. Princes know how to relax, they know how to be comfortable, and, when it comes to dressing, they're more apt to dress down than up.

Most Princesses, by the same token, really aren't into designer clothing and high heels. Their busy lifestyle just doesn't allow for those entrapments. Even though you might find them attired in the workplace as such, it's doubtful that many of them will wear those sorts of things while in relaxation mode. However, it is important to note that Princesses (at least during the courting stage) do tend to dress up more than down.

That's all well and fine. But what does how they dress have to do with hooking them? Everything! We've already established that no one falls in love unless they're absolutely comfortable. And the quickest way to make your love interest antsy—and lose your lure—is to dress in a fashion that throws him or her off kilter. For that reason, toss out everything you ever heard about dressing for love and pay really close attention to this: *People are most relaxed when potential mates mirror their attire.*

This isn't as crazy as it sounds. I once set up a blind date for a very attractive friend of mine. Her work schedule was so heavy that she hadn't dated in quite some time. To say she was excited was putting it mildly; she was absolutely ecstatic. Unfortunately, her mounting excitement got in the way of common sense. Here's what happened.

The date in question was for dinner at a nice steak house, and my friend wanted to make a good impression. She fanned through the closet multiple times and finally came up with four or five outfits she thought would do. Then she called me over to take a look.

I was appalled. Every outfit she'd tossed on the bed was perfectly suited to a black-tie affair. As I put them back in the closet, I explained that her date would probably show up in jeans. This made no impression on her. I explained that she'd be way overdressed. She didn't hear me. As she began pulling the outfits back out of the closet and rummaging around for stiletto heels, rhinestone earrings, and other accoutrements, my final statement of "less is more" fell on completely deaf ears.

The result was disastrous. Her date was so taken aback by her appearance that he could barely speak. In fact, I'm sure he thought about driving away and forgetting the whole thing.

Gentleman that he was, though, he took her to dinner anyway. Much to her dismay, he never called again. She just couldn't understand it. After all, she was certain that she'd made quite the impression.

Fiascos like this don't have to happen to you. In fact, they're very easily avoided. All you need is some common sense and a keen eye. My husband, for example, is a construction superintendent. This means that he's very much at home in jeans and a T-shirt. When we go out, he's very likely to top those jeans with a dress shirt and be done. During the whole of our relationship, I've only seen him don a suit twice, and both times were incredibly special occasions.

Our first date took place at a casual restaurant and was a going-away party for one of his business associates. Because I'd met him before and had never seen him wear anything but jeans, I traded my business attire for denim. The evening was a huge success. He called the next day and arranged a date for the following weekend. Not only did we become inseparable, but he proposed three months later!

Here's the deal: If your love is the suit-wearing type, tailored clothes are the answer. For men, this means jackets, slacks, and the occasional business suit. Women do well with skirts, slacks, blazers, and silk shirts. (*Tip for women:* For sex appeal, leave the top two buttons of your blouse unfastened, then add a strand of pearls or a tasteful necklace.) It's as simple as that.

If your love is the more informal type, work with jeans, slacks, and the occasional jacket or blazer. If pants aren't your thing, ladies, try soft skirts, casual dresses, and denim jumpers. Just remember to keep it simple, because with these folks, simple *is* sexy.

Love Posturing

If your mother was anything like mine, she delivered constant reminders about good posture. "Stand tall," "don't slump," and "sit up straight" were some of her favorite lines. And by the time you were grown, you thought you'd heard everything there was to hear about posture. After all, Mama sang those tunes day in and day out. In fact, she sounded like a broken record.

Unfortunately, though, Mama probably forgot to tell you that posture had anything to do with love or that, used properly, it constitutes the most potent love spell in the world. In fact, it's the one thing guaranteed to cement a relationship quicker than you can say "I do."

Love posturing has very little to do with any of the things that Mama insisted upon. Instead, it has to do with something that probably got you into trouble: a little game called "monkey see monkey do." Simply put, this little trick is a matter of mimicking someone else's gestures. That someone would be your love.

Love posturing can be a little tricky (you certainly don't want to get caught at it!), but it's well worth every effort. Why? Because it takes the comfort zone back to the time of its greatest height—that period of time when we were most comfortable of all: that time before birth, when we were safe and warm in the womb. There was no such thing as personal independence. Everything worked together in one synchronized motion. In fact, we depended on Mama for everything. When she breathed, we breathed. When she ate, we ate. And when she moved, we went along for the ride. We were never left to our own devices; yet we were happier than we've ever been. Although you may never be that comfortable again, your mate will be, provided you master the basics of this very potent magic.

Because perfecting this art takes a little practice, it's best to start with something nearly imperceptible: his or her breathing patterns. The dating game provides lots of opportunities for being really close to each other, so you can get in plenty of practice without being noticed.

The easiest time to try this is while you're snuggled on the couch watching TV. That's because you can actually feel the rise and fall of the chest as your love breathes. Once you've gotten the rhythm down, simply synchronize your breathing to his or hers. Don't worry if you get off track. It's not a problem. Simply start again, and you'll master the technique in no time.

Once you're a synchronized-breathing expert, it's time to graduate to something a little trickier. Begin by taking note of how your love sits: straight or slouched? Legs crossed or with both feet on the floor? What about his or her hands and arms? Are they under the chin, behind the head, or both resting on the legs?

Because the back easily goes unnoticed, start by mimicking its position first. Just straighten or relax, as the case may be. Then go on to the feet and legs, crossing or uncrossing them as necessary. Work with these until you get the hang of it. In a few days, you'll be moving automatically when your love does.

Because hands and arms frequently move toward the face—and we look at the face more often than any other part of the body—they comprise the most difficult part of love posturing. For that reason, be careful when mimicking these movements. You'll need to move slowly, gently, and in one inconspicuous motion. In fact, it's a good idea to wait at least five heartbeats after an initial movement before moving forward with your own. Doing so keeps the motion imperceptible, and that's exactly what you want to accomplish.

Love posturing, though extremely powerful, really isn't difficult. It just takes some time and practice. The results are always worth the effort, though. In fact, the only problem you'll have after mastering its techniques will be getting your love to leave. The object of your affections will be so comfortable with you that he or she will never want to go home again!

Whispering Winds

Now that you've learned some basic skills, it's time to get into the fun stuff: romance. That wonderful combination of fun, seduction, and anticipation that comes from a firm connection between the heart and the mind. When these two begin to communicate, they bring boundless personal energy and a childlike awe to everything that crosses your path. They also bring that funny feeling into the pit of your stomach—the one that makes you think you'll die if you don't hear your love's voice at least 40 times a day and has you watching the clock, pacing the floor, and waiting for that glorious knock on the door.

Chances are, you're already feeling that way. But how do you know if the object of your affections is feeling it, too? More to the point, is there any way you can make sure that your feelings don't go unrequited? Yes! But only if you make it happen. And that comes through mastering the art of seduction.

Seduction isn't what most folks think. It has nothing to do with sex and nudity. Instead, it has to do with what's still covered, what might be underneath, and what comes through loud and clear even when left unsaid. It's a simple matter of what's left to the imagination. Something that results in pure, unadulterated anticipation. It's the same stuff that single-handedly fueled the fire for some of the steamiest relationships in history.

My husband is a pro at seduction. For him, it's not a practiced art. It's not something consciously pondered. In fact, he may not even realize his power. Yet, there it is: strong, true, and undeniable. Even in our whirlwind romance—five months from the first date to the wedding rings—he kept me waiting, imagining, and anticipating. He took his time (at least with the important things).

Although we were in touch every day by phone, we had three dates before he held my hand. Four dates passed before he kissed me goodnight. There were barely audible whispers across the dinner table, mildly suggestive conversations, and nearly imperceptible caresses during romantic movies. In fact, by the time we got around to the "big night," my knees were so weak that I nearly melted right into the floor.

That is seduction. It's that thing that leaves you a little off-kilter and makes your heart pound right out of your chest. It's what leaves you panting, breathless, and begging for more. Seduction is absolutely necessary in every long-term romance. Why? Because without it, nothing in this world will make your pulse race out of control when your mate walks through that door day after day—even after 35 years.

That's all well and fine, but what if you're not like my husband? What if you don't even have the first clue as how to begin? Don't worry. The art of seduction can be learned, practiced, and, with a little patience, mastered. The following tips will get you started.

❧ **Dress seductively.** Frankly, this tip is aimed toward women more than it is toward men. Leave something to the imagination, ladies. For example, two blouse buttons left unfastened is seductive. (Three is not.) A skirt with a slit halfway up the thigh leaves something to the imagination. (A skirt that barely covers the derrière is another story.) The whole idea here is to give your potential mate a chance to imagine what lies beneath the outer covering. That, in itself, is seductive.

❧ **Flirt.** Master flirts never bat their eyelashes, and they'd never dream of using that "I'll bet you're a Taurus" line. In fact, they usually begin from across the room without saying anything at all.

All it takes is subtle but direct smile and a furtive glance or two. What about an opening line? Use your love charm. It's guaranteed to break the ice.

ᚪ **Make eye contact.** There is nothing more seductive than looking into someone's eyes during a conversation. Remember to smile frequently, though. A direct look without a smile is nothing more than staring.

ᚪ **Keep it light.** Really serious conversations have no place in the initial stages of seduction. Instead, try humorous anecdotes that induce laughter. This will keep the conversation going and give you an opening to work with the rest of the process.

ᚪ **Use a gentle touch.** Gentle but spontaneous touching is not only seductive but also perfectly acceptable during casual conversation. Lean in a bit when you talk, then try a quick brush on the arm or a soft pat to the hand when making a point. This will make your partner wonder what it would be like to touch a little more or be a little closer.

ᚪ **Take it slow.** Nothing scares off a potential mate more quickly than coming on too strong. Take everything (with the exceptions of phoning and verbal communications) at least two steps more slowly than you'd like. This gives your partner an opportunity to want more and more until he or she positively craves it. The mind starts to wonder "what if?" The anticipation process kicks in full tilt. Once that happens, the heart overtakes the mind and grabs complete control. The romance of your life is well on the way, and it's all because you had enough restraint to take your time.

Some folks take to the seduction process immediately. In fact, it's as if they were born to be masters of the art. Others, though, are a little more timid. If you fall into the latter group, there's no need for despair. Just try the ritual that follows. It's guaranteed to help you master the art, and once that's done, the rest will be romantic history. Best of all, the object of your affections won't be able to stop thinking of you!

Master-of-Seduction Ritual

For best results, plan to perform this ritual in your bedroom on a Friday when the moon is either waxing or full.

Materials list:

 1 red rose
 1 purple candle
 1 wide-tipped black permanent marker
 Sultry-scented incense (Good choices are
   nag champa, opium, patchouli, and
   myrrh.)

Begin by gathering the materials and taking them to your bedroom. Using the marker, paint the candle black. Cover it completely, including the top and bottom surfaces. Light the incense and watch as its smoke curls into the air. Take note of how the smoke just seems to hang there and linger, evaporating, yet infusing everything in the room with its scent. After a few moments, say:

> I am the incense, whose smoke scents
> the air
> It's like I am present, though I am not
> there

> As smoke curls and rises and then
>   dissipates
> I am the scent which holds open the gates
> Of memory; and through it, I twirl with
>   sheer glee
> Until there is nothing imagined but me

Then pick up the rose and close your eyes. Inhale its heady aroma, and think about the softness of the petals. Think about what it would be like to touch them, caress them, and be totally enveloped in their rich velvet. Inhale again and feel the rose call to you with its own form of seduction. Then open your eyes, look at the rose, and say:

> I am the rose and its heady perfume
> I float on the wind 'neath the Sun and the
>   Moon
> I am the richness of velvet that gently
>   enfolds
> The mind and the heart and the body
>   and soul
> Who long for one simple but gentle
>   caress
> And would count it a measure of
>   greatest success
> As I twirl through the mind without
>   introduction
> I am the rose in its perfect seduction

Place the rose in front of the candle, then light the wick, saying:

As the black burns away and the purple
    appears
My doubts melt away with my personal
    fears
Until all that is left is that which I desire:
A flame that is born of the wick and the
    fire
And dances through hearts without
    great production
I am the master of the art of seduction

Let the candle burn down completely. Place the
rose between your box spring and mattress so it can
work its magic while you sleep.

Romantic Interludes

Although seduction definitely peaks and holds the interest, we just can't fall in love without a hefty dose of romance.
Why? Because romance is the only thing powerful enough
to do the trick. Only romance can sweep us off our feet, give
us wings, and allow us to soar through life without ever touching the ground. It melts our hearts, weakens our constitu-
tions, and makes us feel like kids again. In fact, it's the only
thing in the world that can make life as we know it cease to
exist—and make us like it. Simply put, romance is the stuff
that makes love fun. If it weren't for that, we'd never bother
to fall in love at all.

That being the case, it only makes sense to spend some
time romancing your potential mate. This means some quality
time set aside in romantic planning mode, because real romance
doesn't just happen. In fact, there's nothing spontaneous about

it at all. Romance is premeditated, arranged, and developed. It's calculated, prepared, and maneuvered. It's something that's deliberately delivered for the sole purpose of making your partner's heart go pitter-patter. And it's well worth the trouble.

Take Romeo, for example. He wasn't just passing through the neighborhood when he wound up at Juliette's window. He went there on purpose. That lusciously romantic soliloquy he delivered wasn't any spur of the moment happenstance, either. You can bet your bottom dollar that he rehearsed it at least a hundred times before he left his house, and at least 30 more along the way. Of course, Romeo was a pro. By the time he was done, Juliette wasn't just some dreamy-eyed beauty whose heart was leaping from her chest; she was absolutely drooling over him and completely oblivious to everything else in her life. That's romance, and that's exactly the sort of response you want from your partner.

Admittedly, real romance takes some doing because it involves more than sending a few roses. It's not so hard, though, once you've gotten to know something about your potential mate. It's a simple matter of playing on what your partner likes, adding a few embellishments, and weaving something tailor-made to make him or her feel special.

One of the most romantic dates I ever had began as an early-morning, spontaneous trip to check out some antique shops. Of course, there was nothing spur of the moment about that trip at all. My husband had laid out some very carefully engineered plans. He arranged our outing so that nothing would be open when we arrived. This allowed for a leisurely, romantic walk along the Mississippi River. There was hand-holding, stolen kisses, and more sweet, whispered nothings than I could count on both hands. But that wasn't all: After the walk, he skillfully maneuvered me over to a quilt museum (a place he knew I'd adore), where we spent hours not only entranced by the beauty of color and design but completely enraptured with each other. It was there that I lost my heart.

Please don't misunderstand. There was nothing especially romantic about the museum. There were no candles, no flowers, and no soft, gentle music. It was just a building that housed quilts and didn't lend itself to romance at all. Yet it was there that my heart melted at its very core. Why? Because in taking me there—a place I knew that my husband really didn't give two hoots about—several things became obvious. To start with, nothing really mattered to him but my pleasure. For another, he was interested in the things that made me who I was. Most important, perhaps, was the indication that he was perfectly willing to cultivate whatever was necessary to bring joy to my heart and a smile to my lips. There's nothing in life more romantic than that.

Because romance doesn't always involve something extremely mushy or sappy, it's just not that hard to engineer. Even so, some folks seem to have real trouble with it. I can't even tell you how many times I've given someone romance tips only to hear, "I'm just not that way" or "That's just not *me.*" If you're even thinking of formulating a similar response right now, I have only three words for you: Stop right there.

As uncomfortable as the thought of planning a little romance might be for you, there's definitely something worse: losing the love of your life and watching him or her slip right through your fingers into someone else's. And that's exactly what will happen if you don't get with the program. So swallow your pride and grab some sensitivity. Then try some of the following ideas. No heart in the world can resist!

ငဒ **Send your message in a bottle.** Instead of phoning your love for a date, write the invitation on a piece of paper and roll it tightly into a scroll. Tie it up with red satin ribbon and slip it inside a clean, dry wine bottle. Cork the bottle and tie a note around the neck instructing the recipient to retrieve the message by turning the vessel upside down and tapping firmly on the bottom. (The scroll will fly out, leaving the ribbon inside.) Have the bottle delivered by courier.

ငဒ **Kiss at the movies.** Remember when you were young and the only real reason you went to the movies was to cuddle and kiss your date incessantly? There was something about the darkened movie theater that simply invited that sort of playful romance. No matter how old you are, the same is true today, so don't waste the atmosphere. Make plans to see a romantic movie, then kiss your date long and slow. Don't stop at one or two kisses, though. Rekindle the fires of your teen years and see where it takes you. Don't worry if you miss key portions of the movie. You can always rent it at the video store later!

ငဒ **Cook dinner.** What's romantic about a home-cooked meal? Nothing—unless it's specially prepared for you by the one you love. Invite your love to a quiet dinner at your place. Do it up right with wine, candles, and soft lighting, and arrange your plates so you'll sit close to each other. Because it can be very romantic to feed each other, remember to add some finger foods. Try chocolate covered fruit, cheese-dipped bread, or a variety of bite-sized cheese cubes.

ⓒঽ **Play in the rain.** There's nothing like a nice, warm shower to get rid of all your cares. The same is true of the Spring rains, so invite your love for a nice wet walk. Don't stop there, though. Play and dance. Let the rain unleash the child within. Afterward, dry each other with big, absorbent towels that have been warmed in the dryer or microwave.

ⓒঽ **Have an impromptu picnic.** There's nothing like a picnic to bring out the romantic in everyone. Best of all, you don't need much for this. A bottle of wine, a loaf of bread, and some cheese or fruit will do the trick. Pick a secluded spot under a big tree, spread your blanket, and enjoy each other. If an outdoor picnic isn't an option, just improvise. Simply spread the blanket in your living room and have a picnic there. Sparks will fly. I guarantee it!

ⓒঽ **Snuggle on the couch.** Physical closeness simply invites romance, and except for love-making, nothing brings you closer than good old-fashioned snuggling. Instead of just sitting on the couch side by side to watch TV, position yourself so your back is against the arm of the couch. Then have your love sit between your legs so that his or her back and head rests against your chest. This allows for hair-stroking, shoulder rubbing, and any number of other romantic maneuvers. After a few minutes of this, even the worst movie ever made seems to brim with excitement.

ⓒঽ **Write a poem.** There's nothing quite like a poem to kindle the fires of romance, especially when that poem is written solely for the object of your affections. If you're not the poetic type, try a self-effacing letter. Say everything you haven't had the nerve to say out loud. Then mail it to your love's workplace or send it by courier. Even better, tape it to his or her steering wheel so your love finds it before driving to work.

◁ **Rent a limousine.** Contrary to popular belief, limos are very inexpensive to rent, especially if you only need them for a few hours. And what an impression they make! When a limo arrives to pick up your love for that special dinner or night on the town, hearts are bound to go pitter-patter. Even the neighbors'!

The Magic Words

Three little words—I love you—comprise more magic than any other words in existence. We feel them, we think them, and our actions often mirror them. Sadly enough, though, we frequently have trouble saying them. When that's the case, relationships can end almost before they've begun.

The reasons for the trouble vary. Some folks feel that these words don't have much meaning anymore, and that more often than not, they're used flippantly and insincerely. Others worry that they'll frighten away a potential mate by saying them too quickly. Most folks have another problem: They know that once said, those words are binding. That they signify a commitment of sorts. By their very utterance, they present a point of no return—a point where reciprocal feelings aren't necessarily imminent and where rejection could prevail. It's a very scary place to be. I know, because I've been there.

I'd never put much stock in love at first sight—at least, not until I met my husband. We both wound up at a friend's house for Christmas dinner. One look was all it took. I nearly melted into the floor. Then to complicate things, he gave me a bottle of wine as a thank you gift for signing some books. Of course, that little gesture almost did me in.

My reaction scared the hell out me. It had never happened before, and I wasn't sure what to do with it. Had we been two single people actively searching for love, it would have been different. We weren't, though. I was still involved with someone else.

There were other complications as well. Even if I hadn't already been involved, I knew that I'd never start a relationship with him. There was no way. With his job ending in less than four months, he'd be off to parts unknown. My heart would be broken, and I wasn't going there. I spent the rest of the day trying to get away from him. He spent the rest of the day trying to hold me in conversation. It was a mess, a heart-pounding fiasco that continued for hours after I'd managed to escape.

Fortunately, I got a grip. Life continued normally. Every time the incident managed to infiltrate the recesses of my mind—which it did with regularity—I pushed it back out with a strength I'd never known. All was right with my world, or so I thought.

Then something happened: My long-term relationship fell apart and I moved out. Something happened on my husband's end, too. His job was extended indefinitely. This all happened over the course of seven months. That's when things got scary.

Once we started to date, things took off like a whirlwind. To say that we were incredibly happy was an understatement. We were ecstatic. But that didn't stop the nagging feeling I had inside that things were going too fast and that if I didn't get a handle on them quickly, someone might get hurt. Of course, that someone was me, the practical person who didn't believe that love at first sight was anything more than an illusion. I believed that love (real love, anyway) couldn't possibly blossom that quickly and was afraid of setting my heart up to get broken just one more time.

Then right in the middle of all my confusion, less than two weeks into the relationship, he said them: those three little words that, when all said together in one short sentence, make the world go round. I, who had searched for this sort of love for as long as I could remember, began to fall apart. At first, I tried to talk myself into the fact that I'd misunderstood. This wasn't so hard, because he'd actually whispered them. Just about the time I became thoroughly convinced that such was the case, though, he said them again. This time, there was no mistake. Each word rang out loud and clear.

This presented an awful dilemma for me. I was absolutely certain that he was "the one." Truth be told, I loved him, too. At the same time, though, I'd been burned before by rushing in too quickly, and I remembered it all too well. It certainly wasn't an incident high on my priority list of fun things to do, and I didn't intend to repeat it. With that in mind, I didn't return his declaration of love. Instead, I did nothing except smile.

Some folks might have seen my reaction as a form of rejection and ended the relationship right there. Lucky for me, though, my husband didn't. He simply endured and persisted. Of course, it helped that he could see the big picture. He knew that no matter how you sliced them, things were what they were. This was the real thing, and no matter how stubborn I was or how much I wanted to deny it, I would eventually have to accept that love had not only blossomed in our lives but was dancing in our hearts. He was right. It just took a few more weeks for me to get there.

The point is that fear has no place in the love arena. And if you can't muster the courage to say "I love you"—even when you are head over heels in love—you don't either. Why? Because by the time you get to that point, it's already too late. Your heart's already on the line. It's already reached the point of no return. There's nothing you can do to bring it back into the safety zone. That being the case, you have one of two options: You can either spend the rest of your life alone on the pity pot playing games of "what if?" or you can take a chance. When you examine the options from that angle, the latter is a much better solution.

If that doesn't get you going, think about this: No matter how much you adore someone, there's a distinct possibility that someone else could feel the same way. Would you want to be left out in the cold just because another person beat you to the punch? Certainly not. And that's exactly what could happen if you don't find the words to say how you feel.

Fact is, you have nothing left to lose. Your heart's already put itself at risk. It's already soaring out of control. No amount of begging or pleading is ever going to bring it back, so take a chance. Say those three little words. In doing so, you may discover that they do more than just make your world go round. You may discover that they've just brought your whole world home to you.

That's all well and fine, but what if you're still a little antsy? What if you really want to say how you feel, but the words just won't come? What then? All you need is a shot of courage. The best I've ever found comes from performing the following ritual.

The Shot-of-Courage Ritual

Materials list:

1 yellow candle
1 small piece of turquoise
1 small piece of tigereye
1 small piece of hematite
1 bay leaf
1 pinch cinnamon
1 small drawstring charm bag
(Alternatively, substitute a white handkerchief or a piece of white fabric at least 6 by 6 inches)

Gather the materials and prepare to perform this spell on a Wednesday. (The moon phase doesn't matter for this spell.) Place the materials in front of the candle, then light the candle while seeing yourself not only saying those three little words, but also meeting with a successful reaction. Then hold the turquoise in your hand and say:

> Sarasvati, eloquent One
> Let the words slip from my tongue
> Let them flow with grace and ease
> As I will, so mote it be

Place the stone in the bag (or if you opted for the handkerchief, in the center of the cloth). Then pick up the tigereye and say:

> Ancient Warriors, be my guide
> Bring your courage to my side
> Cast off fear, I beg of Ye
> As I will, so mote it be

Place the stone with the turquoise, pick up the hematite, and say:

> Hematite which grounds and heals
> To your strength, I now appeal
> By the Earth from which you come
> Work your magic—be it done

Place the stone with the others, then place a pinch of cinnamon on top of the bay leaf and say:

> My words with victory shall meet
> Without the prospect of defeat
> My love shall issue forth at last
> With these words the spell is cast

Place the herbs with the stones, draw the bag closed, and knot it. (If you're using a handkerchief, knot it well to secure the ingredients.) Leave the pouch in front of the candle until it burns out, then carry the bag with you. Once you've accomplished the task at hand, bury the charm in the ground.

Chapter Four

Riding Off on the White Horse

nce you have mastered the arts of communication, love posturing, and seduction, it's time to ride off on the proverbial white horse. This does not necessarily mean marriage, but it does offer the opportunity to take your relationship to the next level: that titillating plane of lovemaking. Before you jump into the royal bed, though, there are a few things that you may want to consider, the first of which is that having sex does not necessarily constitute making love.

Is It Sex or Is It Love?

Sex is sex, plain and simple. It's nothing more than the word implies. It's a way to blow off steam, ease tension, and temporarily satisfy physical desire. There's nothing wrong with that. We all have those needs. When you get right down to the bare facts, though, the truth of the matter becomes apparent: You can have hot, passionate, unadulterated sex with anyone. You don't have to be in love. You don't have to like your partner. You don't even have want to see that person the next day, the day after, or the day after that.

Making love is an entirely different story. It's more uplifting than a mood elevator, it's more soothing than a tranquilizer, and it brings more energy and personal gratification than a pound of Godiva's best chocolate truffles. Why? Because couples who are madly in love have something special that simple sex partners do not: Their hearts beat in rhythm and their minds think in sync. More importantly, their spirits soar in unison. When they touch on the physical plane, all three—heart, mind, and spirit—connect.

This all-encompassing connection truly provides the most powerful magic in existence. It can make the whole world go away. It can bring ecstasy beyond your wildest imagination. In fact, it can completely obliterate everything else in your life until nothing exists but the two of you, wrapped in the luscious, passionate rapture of each other's arms. It's nothing short of dynamite. Then in the morning, you'll have that indescribable excitement of finding your love asleep on the pillow next to yours. It's just something that simple sex can't provide.

First-Time Villains

Making love with a new partner for the first time can be the most fabulous thing in the world—if you're absolutely sure that both of you are ready. Even so, the very thought can stir up some really sticky situations. For one thing, you're probably nervous. You've never been together before, you don't know your love's personal likes and dislikes, and you certainly don't want to do anything to screw things up. First-time jitters are normal. If that's all that's wrong, there is absolutely nothing to worry about.

Unfortunately, though, other villains tend to call on both parties at this point, and they don't go away easily. In fact, they're not only rude in their intention to stay, but they can be downright mean and hateful. They gleefully point out every physical imperfection you've ever been concerned with, then magnify it times three. Just to make sure that you got the point, they toss in a hefty dose of performance anxiety. Before they're done, you're too terrified to even leave the house, much less take off your clothes.

Body Issues

Women tend to worry about their bodies more than anything else when it comes to first-time love-making. They stand naked in front of the mirror and sort through every imperfection. Whether it's sagging breasts or back-of-the-leg cellulite, women see it. They magnify it. Then they blow it so out of proportion that there's no room in the mirror for anything that's right. And that's no way to embark on a journey that could be the most passionate ride of their lives!

Whether they're overweight, too thin, or the cellulite queen of the universe, ladies need to keep one thing in mind: Your Prince is absolutely crazy about you—the real you—the one who stole his heart. He truly doesn't care if you have a few physical imperfections. His infatuation with you alone is more than enough to turn him on. Besides, a flawlessly perfect body could just scare the hell out of him.

Here's the deal: Although men may like to look at the latest centerfold, they recognize a fantasy when they see one. They realize that real women simply aren't built that way. More to the point, they're glad of it. Why? For one thing, men don't really like hard muscle tone and sharp angles when it comes to making love. They like curves, softness, and the gentle touch that only real women can supply. What's more, when they wake up in the morning after a passionate night of ecstasy, they want it all over again. It's something that a centerfold model, no matter how gorgeous or perfect, just can't provide.

The other reason that men don't usually go for women who look like centerfolds is because such perfection presents some heart-wrenching worries. First and foremost, there's the worry that his body isn't as flawless as hers. There's the worry of being the perfect lover and being able to satisfy her. Put it all together, and you have a huge rejection complex in the making. Before it's said and done, a hefty case of performance anxiety sets in. The last thing he wants to do is make love. In fact, he couldn't even if he wanted to.

Size Issues

Because we're on the subject of men, it's probably a good idea to address that really sticky issue that guys seem to ponder more than anything else. That particular issue, of course, has to do with size.

For some unknown reason, size seems to cause more worry and angst among men than anything else on the planet. Even the possibility of another world war doesn't undo them quite as badly. Think I'm kidding? Just deliver one off-handed size-related comment and see what happens. Men go straight into orbit, and plaster themselves to the ceiling. Once they're peeled off (and picked up from the floor), most lapse into self-examination mode. They stare directly at their crotches as if some alien life-form is housed within. Others just fall apart. There is no physiological reason for these sorts of reactions; it's simply the villain at work.

Size does matter—but only to the villain. He tells you that bigger is better, that you—as well as the entire female population—would be much happier if you only had another inch or two. After all, you'll never be able to satisfy *anyone* with the equipment you currently possess. Then the villain delivers the final blow: He convinces you that other men, normal ones anyway, can actually wrap their penises around their waists and stick them in their ears. It's enough to make anyone crazy.

Here's the deal: It doesn't matter whether you have four inches, nine inches, or possess the equipment of a porn star.

Why? Because delivering the orgasm of a lifetime has absolutely nothing to do with your size. To start with, women much
prefer someone who's not too large. That way, they can relax
and enjoy themselves. (There's nothing worse than being
smack-dab in the throes of passion only to become suddenly
inhibited by the fear of pain.) The other thing is that for
women, love-making is an emotional event. This means that
treating her in bed as if she were the Goddess incarnate is the
sexiest thing you can ever do for her. It's that attitude, that
willingness to please her right into ecstatic oblivion, that will
bring her to heights she's never experienced. She'll not only
love you for it, but she won't be able to take her hands off of
you.

Pre-Jitters-Eradication Ritual

Some folks have an awful time controlling the fears from
first-time jitters. If that's the case with you, just try the following ritual. It's quick, it's easy, and, once performed, nothing
will enter your mind but the delicious ecstasy that awaits you.

Although this ritual is very effective when performed on
the day that you intend to make love, most of us don't have
that luxury. That's because first-time love-making is usually
a spontaneous act, and we just don't know for sure when it's
likely to happen. That being the case, it's a good idea to
perform this ritual as quickly as possible.

There's no need to worry about day of the week
or moon phase here. Just grab a white candle and a
black permanent marker and head for the nearest
full-length mirror in your house. (If you don't have a
full-length mirror, work in front of the bathroom or
dresser mirror, whichever is largest.)

Using the marker, color the candle black just as you did in the Master-of-Seduction Ritual previously. Then take several deep breaths and clear your mind. Light the candle and firmly say:

> As this wax, the flame does sear
> Imperfections disappear
> And with them go anxiety,
> Stress and nervous energy
> Until the only thing I wear
> Is the joy and passion that I'll share
> With my love in ecstasy
> When we are one—all else must flee

Then visualize all your doubts and fears as if they are cords plugged into your body from a main power source. Pull each plug first from the power source and then from the point of connection to your body. (It's important to do this not only in the correct order, but also to disconnect both ends; otherwise, the cords will be able to attach themselves to you again.) As you see each cord fall, say:

> Gone is your matrix and source of
>   supply
> Your power is gone—you must shrivel
>   and die

Close your eyes and spend a few moments visualizing your partner finding you perfect in every way. Let the candle burn all the way down.

The Big Night

No matter how much we want the first time to fulfill our every romantic fantasy, sometimes it just doesn't work out that way. In fact, it often plays more like an episode of *The Three Stooges* than a steamy love scene from *Romeo and Juliet.* I've experienced everything from an overly ardent pet bouncing into the bed to the jangle of an overactive smoke alarm. The worst, however, was the time that an ill-placed kiss caused an involuntary knee-jerk, and my partner's nose was history!

When these things happen (and they do) love-making is pretty well done for the evening. There's no need to be upset or put the night to rest, though. Just treat the incident with humor. Laugh—not just a nervous giggle, but right out loud. Because laughter is contagious, you're partner will laugh, too. The rest of the evening can be spent in romantic cuddle mode. Who knows? The night could still provide the most romantic memory you'll ever know—all because you had the good sense to break the tension.

Although you can't always prevent things from going awry on that special night, there are a few things you can do to ensure that your partner is relaxed and receptive. Some tips are for men, some are for women, and others work equally well for both. For your convenience, we'll start with the things that apply to both parties.

Tell Me Truly

Honesty is always a good policy, but it's especially true in the bedroom. Why? Because your partner isn't a mind reader and can't possibly know what you enjoy unless you put it into words. Unfortunately, many people just aren't comfortable talking about their sexual likes and dislikes, especially on the first night. If you're one of those people, stop right there and ask yourself the following questions:

- ᘓ Do I want to feel loved and appreciated?

- ᘓ Do I want to enjoy sex with my partner?

- ᘓ Do I want to reach peaks of ecstasy that I've never dreamed possible?

If the answer to any of these questions is yes, then you're going to have to talk about it. It's not so hard. You just have to open your mouth and let the words come tumbling out. Still, some people have trouble with this. If you're one of those people, all is not lost. Just turn the tables. Ask your partner about personal fantasies and turn-ons. Once the answers start to flow, you won't feel so self-conscious, and you will be better able to express your own likes and dislikes.

These conversations are probably the most important that you'll ever initiate with your love, for they not only set the stage for tonight's activities, but for any intimacy thereafter. For this reason, it pays to be graphically honest. Don't worry that your partner will think you're kinky or prudish. This isn't just sex you're talking about; it's love-making. Anything that makes you feel loved is worth discussing. Besides, if you start your sexual relationship with honesty, you'll never have to worry about shaky ground, at least not in the bedroom.

Erogenous Zones

Although most people automatically think in terms of genital areas when it comes to erogenous zones, those spots only comprise a small part of the whole picture. Simply put, an erogenous zone is any place where nerve endings form close to the skin surface. The body is just full of them. Sadly enough, though, we tend to ignore everything but the genitals, and, in doing so, we miss out on what could be the most delicious experiences in romantic ecstasy. For that reason, I urge you to explore all the areas listed here *before* genital stimulation. By the time you get there, your partner will be absolutely writhing from pleasure and anticipation!

- **Scalp.** There is nothing quite as sensual as the feeling of fingers gently running through the hair. A soft, gentle circular motion at the base of the skull can be quite titillating, too.

- **Ears.** Try slowly running your finger along the curve behind the ear while tracing its inner curvature with your tongue. Take your time and go slowly. It's simply delicious!

- **Neck.** This is one of the most sensitive areas of the body. Light, feathery kisses and the gentle movement of your tongue can bring your partner to new heights.

- **Shoulders and collarbone.** Gently trace these areas slowly and deliberately with the tip of one finger. The tip of your tongue works well, too.

- **Arms.** These hold, perhaps, the most ignored erogenous zone of the body. The inner arm and underarm areas are extremely sensitive when stimulated with light, gentle touches.

- **Hands and fingers.** Start by softly running your fingers over your partner's, then trace the palm area with one fingertip. Lightly kiss the end of each finger. Slide your tongue from the finger base to the tip, and end by taking each finger in your mouth and gently sucking its length.

- ℭ𝔰 **Nipples.** Nipple stimulation can be tremendously exciting for both partners, especially when performed with the light, circular motion of a fingertip or tongue. (Men's nipples are extremely sensitive, so a gentle touch is very important here. The last thing you want to do is make them sore!)

- ℭ𝔰 **Navel.** Trace the outer perimeter with your finger or tongue. For added pleasure, fill the center with something delectable and lick it out.

- ℭ𝔰 **Buttocks.** Light, feathery touches and gentle massaging goes a long way toward heightened foreplay. The line between the buttocks is especially sensitive. Use your finger to gently trace the area from the point of origin to the inner thigh and back up again.

- ℭ𝔰 **Inner thigh.** Use your fingertip or tongue to massage this area in small circular movements. Remember to avoid the genital area.

- ℭ𝔰 **Feet and toes.** Although these areas can be massaged with the fingers and tongue much like the hands and fingers, it's much more pleasurable and exciting to massage them with something else. Use your imagination.

Because everyone's different, the same things that feel good to one person might not appeal to another. For that reason, it's important to pay close attention to your partner's responses during erogenous exploration. Soft moans and slight quivers are a good indication of enhanced pleasure. If your partner suddenly draws you away from any particular area, pay heed. Just continue the discovery phase in another zone. You'll be glad you did.

First-Night Tips for Men

No matter how experienced you are in the arts of love-making (or how successfully you performed the Pre-Jitters-Eradication Ritual earlier in this chapter) this night will be like no other. That's because you have no idea what your love really expects of you. All you have to go on is what she's said. And you know just as well as I do that sometimes, what she doesn't say is just as important. This can prove to be very confusing. Confused is the one thing you don't want to be when you're wrapped up in her arms.

Fortunately, there's a simple solution. All you have to do is treat every portion of her body as if it's the most delectable morsel you've ever beheld. Then look straight into her eyes. Tell her how much you adore her, how beautiful she is, and how good it feels to hold her.

Doing this with sincerity causes a chain reaction that's well worth the effort. First she'll relax, because women (whether they want to admit it or not) really don't want to be in bed with anyone who doesn't adore them. Second, her body issues will fly right out the window. Third and most important, though, she'll feel free to release all the emotion she's been storing inside. Once that happens, she'll respond to you in a way you never dreamed possible.

First-Night Tips for Women

If your man has been honest with you about what he likes, your problems are solved, right? Yes—as long as he was completely forthcoming and other issues didn't get in the way. However, most men are much more timid than women when it comes to discussing their feelings, and you can double that shyness when the discussion at hand involves feelings associated with sexual gratification.

The reasons are many. To start with, most men are brought up to believe that any show of emotion or admittance of "need" is a sign of weakness. And though this is gradually changing, your chances of having hooked a man who has a complete and total disregard for this idea are slim indeed. Some men also believe that certain topics of conversation are taboo with women, and sexual gratification measures top the list. There are also those men who believe that their partner should automatically know what turns them on. I could go on and on, but you get the idea. The bottom line is that you may not have much to work with when it comes to making him feel more loved than anyone else on the planet.

But before you throw up your hands, tear out your hair, or run screaming from the room and forget the whole idea, I have two little words for you: Enjoy yourself. These words are simple to understand and even easier to put into practice. Best of all, they'll guarantee you both the best night of love-making you've ever had.

There's nothing more exciting to a man than a woman who's enjoying herself when making love, especially when he's the object of her pleasure. Why? Because if she's having a good time, he knows that he's doing something right. All self-confidence issues sail right out the window. With those out of the way, everything else goes, too. There's nothing on his mind but you: the woman who's enjoying him. And when he gets to that point, he'll definitely feel loved. Best of all, you'll both reap the benefits.

The Rule of Three

I once heard that when making love with a new partner, the first three times didn't count. The more I mulled it over, the more sense it made. Body issues, size issues, and pre-jitters aside, it takes a little time to get to know each other on such an intimate level. It takes awhile to settle in and be comfortable. You can't, after all, expect your love to read your mind, know what you need, or understand every personal fantasy after one intimate encounter. Doing so just isn't fair.

The point is this: Although it's human nature to draw immediate conclusions about everything else in life, jumping the gun in this area could be a very big mistake. Why? Because life being what it is, things are bound to go awry occasionally. And if you base a decision on what's gone wrong (especially after only a few encounters) you could possibly miss out on the most delightfully sensual love you've ever made.

Do yourself a favor: Give your sexual relationship some time to develop. If something's missing, say so. If you want something that you're not getting, admit it. Chances are, your partner's feeling the same way but just hasn't found the words yet. So initialize the conversation if necessary, then work through the issues gently and lovingly.

Above all else, strike the first three times from your mind. They're absolutely no indication of what's to come. Just handle this area of your relationship with as much tender loving care as you have the other aspects. The results will be more than you've ever imagined. Before all is said and done, you'll both be breathless and begging for more!

Moonlight and Roses

After the first few nights together, you should be feeling much better. And why not? Those intimate concerns are gone. The villains who brought them to the forefront are yesterday's news, and with those out of the way, you can finally relax. All that's left to do is to embrace your relationship and enjoy each other's company. This is a good thing.

Unfortunately, though, there is such a thing as being too comfortable, especially when it comes to building a solid relationship. That's because relationships take work. And when we get too comfortable, we tend to forget about the important things, those delightfully fun little things—seduction, romance, and good old-fashioned flirting—that brought you together in the first place. Those are the very things that make the difference between a simple fling and the once-in-a-lifetime relationship you've been dreaming of.

For that reason, it pays to stay on your toes and look for ways to keep your relationship fresh and exciting. Otherwise, romance stagnates. Boredom sets in. Before you know it, you start to think that your love—that wonderfully exciting thing that made life worth living—has gone by the wayside. It's not a fun place to be. Fortunately, this sort of thing is easily prevented. All it takes are a little thought and minimal effort.

My husband, for example, always brings flowers to the airport when he comes to pick me up. I, on the other hand, see to it that he has a card for every day I'm gone from home. Neither takes much time. Neither is much trouble. Both are things that make us feel loved and appreciated. Because of that sort of effort, our romance is just as new today as it was the day it began. In fact, we fall in love all over again every single day. It's the most wonderful thing in the world.

There are literally tons of ways to keep your love in bloom. I've found that one of the most effective, though, is to set the stage first by performing the spell below. Once performed, the heart seems to soar, and finding ways to keep romance blossoming doesn't seem to present a problem.

Basil Love Spell

Materials list:

    6 basil seeds
    1 cup warm water
    1 4-inch pot
    6-inch square piece of white paper
    Sterile soil
    Colored marking pens

On the Thursday closest to the full moon, place the basil seeds in a cup of warm water and say:

> Oh, Great Aphrodite, hear my plea
> Bring germination to these seeds
> As they steep in this water, let love
>   steep in our hearts
> Bringing both seeds and romance a
>   wondrous new start

Allow the seeds to steep overnight.

The next day, gather the pot, soil, paper, and marking pens. Draw a heart in the center of the paper, add some flowers and smiley faces, then color them. Fold the paper into thirds, then into thirds again. Place the paper in the bottom of the pot and say:

With our love, I make this bed
So romance blossoms in our heads
And in our hearts, its happy tune
Shall rise anew with Sun and Moon

Fill the pot with soil and plant the seeds, and say with each one:

Oh seeds of love and romance grow
Dig deep your roots in soil below
Sprout and green—be lush and thrive
Grow tall and fragrant—come alive
For romance blossoms as you sprout
And fills our lives within and out

Water the seeds, then keep them in a sunny spot in your house. Repeat the last chant daily until they begin to sprout. Tend the plants regularly, and give them a fertilizer stick once every couple of months.

Romantic Fertilizers

There are lots of ways to keep love growing, thriving and blossoming. It's a simple matter of having the right mindset. All you have to do is think "romance." If you performed the preceding spell, that really shouldn't be a problem. Should your idea pool happen to run dry, though, don't worry. Just try some of the following tips. They'll not only flood the pool again, but they'll keep love flowing in ways that you never dreamed possible.

ග **Lunchbox notes.** There's nothing like a little love in the middle of the day to keep things on a happy note. Leave a note in your love's lunchbox. Better yet, write "I love you" on a piece of paper, cover it in plastic wrap, and place it inside a sandwich. It's something your partner will remember for years to come.

ග **Coupon booklets.** Have you ever wanted your partner's complete and undivided attention but didn't quite know how to get the point across? Chances are your love has the same problem. This is where the coupon booklet comes in. Just write out some coupons on small slips of paper for whatever services you'd like to offer (anything from foot rubs to passionate kisses to wild sex; your only limit is the scope of your imagination). Then staple them together, place them in an envelope, and put them on your partner's pillow. He or she will use every one of them. I guarantee it!

ග **Bathing adieux.** Bathing together keeps romance exciting. The key here, though, is in the element of surprise, so give your partner a few minutes before joining him or her. If baths are more to your liking (and your tub is large enough) try adding two or three packets of strawberry gelatin to the water before calling your partner in to join you. It's a sensuous treat that you'll both enjoy.

ග **Treasure hunts.** Remember how much fun these were when you were a kid? The same can be true of adulthood—especially when love is involved. Write a very self-effacing, soul-baring love letter and hide it somewhere on the premises. (Hiding it on your body can be fun, too!) Then write out a series of directional clues and place them in various spots around your house. Give the first clue to your love and see how long it takes to unearth the treasure.

‿ৎ **Flower power.** Contrary to popular belief, men enjoy getting flowers just as much as women do. With that in mind, surprise your love with a fragrant bouquet. If you are short on cash, don't worry. Flowers don't have to come from the florist to touch the heart. Just grab some from the grocery store and watch your love's eyes light up.

‿ৎ **Love mail.** It's always nice to get something in the mail other than bills. But when it's an expression of love from your partner, it can fill even the dreariest day with sunshine. In fact, it can make you feel 10 feet tall! Find a romantic card, add a personal message, and send it to your love's workplace. It will single-handedly rebuild that first-love anticipation, so much so, in fact, that your partner won't be able to wait to see you again!

‿ৎ **Phone romance.** A phone call doesn't take much time, but it often goes a long way toward keeping romance in blossom. Take a minute and pick up the phone. Call just to say "I love you," "I miss you," or maybe even "I hope you took your vitamins, because you'll need all the strength you can muster tonight!" Your love will be walking on air all day.

Thorns in the Garden

Because love is like a rose garden, thorns are bound to crop up now and then. And no matter how much you adore each other or how perfectly suited you are, these nasty little critters can eventually pierce your happiness. At first, there's just a prick. Then a drop of blood. Ignore them and things really get vicious. Before it's said and done, there's a wound so raw, so gaping, and so festered that no amount of love in the world can heal its pain. One of two things is then inevitable: a silence so thick you can cut it with a knife or a screaming match to end all others. No matter how you slice it, you and yours simply refuse to play nice. In fact, you refuse to play at all.

This doesn't have to happen to you. All that's necessary is a bit of strategic pruning: a precisely placed snip here and there to keep the thorns from getting out of hand. And keeping them under control isn't as difficult as you may think.

The first order of business is to remember that we are all products of our life experiences. Because relationships figure into all areas of our lives, we truly are comprised of the lessons learned from people we've allowed into our intimate circle. This means that we judge all actions (and the effects thereof) by some other action within our experience. Although this may not be the most sensible way to handle life, it's the only protection device we have at our disposal.

Here's how it works: When something happens to us, good or bad, we look for a cause. Of course, this is usually the last thing that happened before the outcome. Once we connect the cause and effect, we bundle them together in a neat little package. Then we store it away in the memory bank for future reference. In short, we create an emotional button.

Sometimes these buttons are pushed without warning. Mostly, though, they are pushed without reason. Someone says or does something. A button comes to the forefront. Because it's there, we not only assume the same outcome, but we begin to prepare for it. It's a simple matter of human nature. Unfortunately, it's not fair.

Let's say, for example, that an ex-love once phoned to cancel a date. You didn't think it was any big deal, because the conflict was work-related. The next day, though, you discovered that the object of your affections wasn't really working at all. Instead, he or she was out on the town romancing someone else.

Now your new love calls with a cancellation. The reason is more than sound. Do you listen to the explanation? Do you even bother to see what happens? No. Instead, the red flag pops up. The button flies to the surface. Before you know it, everything connected to that past experience rises from the ashes and pushes the button with a good, strong thud. You decide that you're done. The relationship is over because something as silly as a past experience overshadowed your good judgment.

This is not to say that we shouldn't pay attention when something doesn't ring true. But neither can we live our lives just waiting for the other shoe to fall—at least, not without good reason. So how do we keep life experience from ruining our relationships? More to the point, how do we keep our emotional buttons in check without destroying them entirely?

First, we have to remember that everyone is different. No one ever acts or reacts identically in the same set of circumstances. Second, it's important to note that the current object of your affections didn't create the button that dealt you so much misery. Finally, we have to remember that he or she only pushed the button inadvertently. How could it be otherwise? Your current love, after all, didn't even know that the button existed.

That said, take some time to look at the remedies that are listed here. When thorns crop up (and they will now and then) these simple solutions will go a long way toward preventing undue damage. Used frequently, they'll also keep that stabbing effect far away from your heart.

- ᵴ **Be calm.** Think the situation through and view it with a rational eye. In doing so, you may discover that there really isn't a problem at all other than the fact your buttons are too sensitive. If that's the case, blow it off. Understand that it's time for some long overdue personal healing.

  If that's not the case, take some time to collect your wits. Know that others listen to those who remain calm and that your message will come through much more clearly if you deliver it with rationality.

- ᵴ **Think before you speak.** This is important because most folks will say anything when they're hurt or angry—and the more offensive, the better. Remember that once you've said it, you can't take it back. It's already hit its mark and created a wound. For that reason, only say what you mean; if anything else dares to surface, just choke it back into silence.

- ᵴ **Talk it out.** There is nothing like a good old-fashioned talk to straighten things out, especially when you speak in the unique terms your love understands. (For more information, see the section on love matches in Chapter 3.) This doesn't

mean that you'll agree with everything your partner has to say, but the interchange will definitely
provide you both with necessary information. First,
you'll be able to see where your partner is coming
from. More important, though, it may just provide
you with the insight necessary to keep the relationship growing smoothly.

⍟ **Use love posturing.** There's more to this posture
thing than monkey-see-monkey-do. If you need to
say something that your partner may find objec-
tionable, it's a good idea to disassociate yourself
from the remark somewhat. Just rise from your
seat, go to another part of the room, and say what
needs to be said. Then return to your seat when
your partner speaks. This posturing works like a
subliminal message and provides some neutral
ground. Although the remark is out in the open
(and your partner must consider it) it will seem to
have dropped into the conversation all by itself.
Your partner will associate it with the discussion
,but never as having come from your mouth.

⍟ **Keep your voice low.** Screaming will automatically
put your partner on the defensive, and that's a
place you don't want to go—especially if you think
the relationship is still worthwhile. Instead, make
a conscious effort to lower your voice. Doing so
will keep things on an even keel while you work
toward sorting them out.

⍟ **Diffuse the anger.** This emotion—though it may
be completely justified—can spell trouble when
it comes to sorting things out. Why? Because it's
nearly impossible to see the whole picture when

anger is involved. All you can think about is how ticked off you are, how much you've been hurt, and how much you'd really enjoy strangling your mate if just given half a chance. That being the case, you can forget about a solution. There is a way to get around this, though. Simply visualize a pink heart on the chest of the angry party (yourself, if necessary). Then carefully remove the lower right hand quadrant in your mind's eye. Hold the image for a few minutes, and things will calm down immediately.

ভ **Compromise.** Regardless of what's happened, remember that living life has nothing to do with the hands it deals us. Instead, it's all about how we play the game, so it pays to practice the art of compromise. You don't have to lose yourself in the deal, though, or take any stand that makes you feel uncomfortable. Just give a little. You'll be amazed at how much that one small concession can go toward straightening out a potentially damaging situation and at how much you may gain in return.

ভ **Be willing to forgive.** Remember that no one—not even Prince Charming or Princess Perfect—comes into this world without flaws. If that were the case, he or she wouldn't be human. Be magnanimous enough to accept a forthcoming apology. And whatever you do, don't file the episode away as future ammunition. Just release it and go on. It's the best way to move forward in your relationship and guarantee a happy life.

There are times when couples simply can't work things out for themselves. Should you fall into that category, don't hesitate. Go for help. Find a mediator in the form of a mutual friend or a certified counselor. It may just take an objective viewpoint to straighten out your troubles—troubles that no amount of personal conversation can tackle.

Smoothing Ruffled Feathers

Even when uncomfortable situations are discussed, straightened out, and put to bed, there are times when one or both partners have trouble forgetting the problem. One or both partners still feel some pang of annoyance or hurt feelings. There's no real reason for it. After all, everything's been forgiven. The pain is still there, though, and left untended, it can cause a real rift in even the most loving of relationships. This phenomenon is commonly known as ruffled feathers.

I have to admit that I'm no stranger to this occurrence. In fact, my feathers get ruffled more quickly than most, especially when I've been accused of something that I didn't do. It's not something I can help. Unfortunately, it's just a part of my personal makeup. What I do know, though, is that I can't go through life with a chip on my shoulder—and certainly not where matters of the heart are involved.

So what do I do? More to the point, how do I get over it?

If I'm the only one who can't forget, there's nothing I can do but take responsibility for my feelings. Simply put, I have to release them. That's not always as easy as it sounds, though, because feelings simply aren't tangible. There's seldom any rhyme or reason behind them. That being the case, just grabbing them and tossing them out isn't a real possibility.

That's where the following ritual comes in. It's quick, it's easy, and it tackles this phenomenon more efficiently than anything else on the magical market. Give it a shot. See how quickly your feathers fall back into place and how soon you're back on track to being the sleek, happy lovebird you were born to be.

Hurt-Feelings-Be-Gone Ritual

Materials list:

    1 wide-tipped black permanent marker
    Bright-colored wax crayons
    White paper
    Fireproof dish

With this ritual, there's no need to worry about the phase of the moon or day of the week; it works quickly regardless of the magical conditions. In fact, it's best to perform it just as soon as ruffled feathers come into play.

Begin by taking your materials to a quiet place where you won't be disturbed. In fact, you may want to turn off the phone's ringer, because nothing dashes concentration like a constant jangling in your ear. With this ritual, total concentration is paramount to success.

Place the paper on a hard surface and open the crayon box. Starting with the brightest color available, begin to scribble on the paper. It's important to note here that this work of art need not be pretty. This is chaos you're creating: a mirror of all the emotional anxiety that you feel inside. Be bold and erratic in your strokes.

Choose another color and think about all the hurt you feel inside. Say:

> I am hurting—I feel bad
> I am pissed off—I'm damned mad
> And as I color on this page
> I bring to vision all my rage

Still concentrating on your anxieties and continuing the chant, choose another color, then another, and another, until the entire page is completely covered in crayon marks. When you're satisfied with the page, pick up the magic marker and draw a large black X (from corner to corner) across the paper and say:

> I cancel anxiety—I cancel out rage
> I cancel hurt feelings with the X on this
>   page

Rip up the paper and place the pieces in the fireproof dish. Set them on fire and say:

> I burn away all residue
> To harmful thoughts, I bid adieu
> They're gone forever from my life
> And with them, go all stress and strife

When the ashes cool, scatter them on the winds or bury them outdoors.

Performing this ritual is well and fine if you are the injured party. What if your partner is the one who can't seem to put things in perspective, though? What then? Thankfully, there's help, but it's not as easy as performing a simple spell. In fact, you may have to really work hard at setting things right.

What's really in order here is a bit of molly-coddling. Simply put, you're going to have to do some major sucking up. No matter how much you may hate the thought of that, it's best to start right away. Just remember that when you have to eat crow, it goes down much better if it's still warm.

Begin with a very sincere apology; in this case, a half-hearted one won't do. Tell your partner that you would walk over hot coals if it would make the whole mess go away. (It doesn't matter that it won't. Just hearing that will make your partner feel better.) Tell your partner that you would never in a million years hurt his or her feelings on purpose and that your love is just as deep as it ever was. Then, as a last resort and only if nothing else seems to work, go on and use the F word. That's right: Say you were a fool, and get it over with.

By this time, your partner should be in the perking-up stages. This is a good thing, because it means that you're making progress. Unfortunately, though, this is no time to dispense with the molly-coddling. In fact, you're just getting started.

Go on to ask your love what you can do to make things better. Listen very carefully to what comes out of his or her mouth. If it's humanly possible (and reasonable), you owe it to the relationship to take a stab at getting it done. (Incidentally, a real Prince or Princess will never ask you to do something totally humiliating. If that's the case, you only have a Frog in royal clothes, and it's best to get rid of the critter posthaste!)

Once you've taken care of that, go on to the next phase. Declare one of the next three days as his or her day and plan something that your love really enjoys. This could be a special meal, an outing to a favorite place, or a good old-fashioned back rub. You might buy a small gift as a peace offering, write a romantic poem, or send flowers. (Considering whether your partner is a lover of sight, sound, or emotion will lend some help here.) Whatever you decide is fine as long as you do something with only your partner in mind. Then really spend the day pampering your love. Things will be back to normal before you know it.

Ruffled Feathers Prevention Spell

Because molly-coddling isn't fun—and crow never appears high on a list of delectable edibles—you may want to prevent this sort of thing altogether. The best way to accomplish that is to perform the following ritual on the next full moon.

Materials list:

1 small piece of jet
1 purple candle
1 envelope (business-sized or No. 10)
1 bird feather (Any feather will do as long as it comes from a gentle species. Dove, sparrow, wren, or canary feathers are ideal. Feathers from the blue jay, mockingbird, and crow will only complicate things, as will those from predator birds such as the owl, hawk, or kestrel.)

Begin by placing the candle behind the stone, feather, and envelope. Light it and say:

Purple power lit with fire
Bring me now what I desire:
Prevention of all ruffled feathers
To keep our love from stormy weather

Pick up the feather and, being careful not to burn yourself, move it in a circular, clockwise motion around the candle flame. Then blow on the feather and say:

> Gift of feathered, gentle creature
> Breathe new life and be our teacher
> Guide us with your joy and peace
> And bring our love your happy ease

Place the feather in the envelope and pick up the stone. Hold the stone to your forehead and visualize your relationship as being calm and happy. Moving the stone around the candle flame in the same fashion as the feather, say:

> Solid gift of Air and Fire
> And Water, heed now my desire
> Lend your power and erase
> All ruffled feathers—leave no trace
> Preventing all returning flight
> By warmth of day and cool of night

Put the stone in the envelope and seal it. Lick your finger and use it to trace a heart on the back of the parcel, then place it in front of the candle. Once the candle burns out, center the envelope between your mattress and box springs.

Chapter Five

Living in the Castle

once heard a woman say that she thought marriage would be like having a lifelong date. At first, I laughed and muttered that she must have lost her mind, but then I settled down and really thought about what she'd said. For the first time, I realized that I, too, had once thought the very same thing.

Of course, this gave me pause for thought. I began to wonder if we were the only two people on the planet who had ever employed this line of thinking. After talking to lots of other people in committed relationships, though, I was amazed at the findings. Nearly every one of them—at one point or another in their relationships—had shared the same thought as well. Most were extremely disappointed to discover that such was not the case.

So, how do we get this crazy idea? Where does it come from? More to the point, how can we—obviously intelligent human beings—embrace this fallacy without checking it out first?

The answer is simple: We're in love.

I've often said that if we could develop a system to force the heart and mind to work together, it would be worthy of the Nobel Prize. Unfortunately, it will never happen. Maybe that's not such a bad thing. People who enter into long-term relationships have at least two things going for them. Yes, they're in love, but, more important, they're still in infatuation mode. It's the latter that makes the thought of a lifelong commitment not only plausible but extremely enjoyable. In fact, if it weren't for infatuation, the whole idea of committed relationships would simply cease to exist, and the human race would be a very unhappy sort, indeed.

Infatuation occurs when the heart and mind refuse to work together, and to a large degree this makes the world go round. While we're under its spell, we become oblivious to everything except the fact that we're in love. We don't see minor character flaws. We discount habits that could annoy us in years to come. We even think that we can single-handedly change the world. Thus it's an absolute given that we could change our mates should they suddenly stumble into a state of imperfection.

When we enter into a long-term relationship, though, other things quickly come into view: dirty socks and underwear, toothpaste tubes squeezed from the wrong end, or maybe even shoes in the middle of the living room floor.

Other aggravations enter the picture, too. There are bills to pay, calls to make, errands to run. There are dentist appointments to schedule, piles of dirty dishes to wash, and toilets to clean. Right in the middle of it all, your mate calls to see if you can handle one more little thing. Just at that exact moment, the dog—who's always been the most docile and gentle soul imaginable—decides to detain the postal worker by grabbing his pants leg and baring her teeth. It's enough to make you crazy, but there's nothing you can do. It's a simple matter of mundanity at work. And whether we like it or not, mundanity is where we really live.

Long-term relationships seldom meet our initial expectations, but this doesn't mean that you should avoid entering into one—or that the romance you've cherished so much will fly right out the window. What it does mean is that you should go into it with a realistic eye and understand that sharing your lives takes things to a different level—a more comfortable level where only perfect trust and true love can flourish.

I'll never forget a conversation my husband initiated early in our relationship. He announced that someday, he'd ask me to marry him. I remember telling him that for me, marriage had always meant losing a really good boyfriend, and because of that, I just couldn't see the point. His response was that marriage to the right person could be a wonderful thing and that there was something not only reassuring but exciting about the monogamous relationship. It meant having someone special to come home to, someone fun to share life's experiences with, and someone wonderful to simply cuddle up with night after night.

Once I began to look at it from that angle, marriage didn't seem like such a bad thing at all. In fact, it took on a whole new light. I suddenly realized that my view of marriage had been flavored by unrealistic expectations—expectations that had nothing to do with real life—and as a result, I'd never found the happiness it offered. It was a mistake I vowed never to make again.

Even so, I have to admit that I was more than just a little nervous the night before our wedding. In fact, I stayed awake for hours playing the "what if?" game and worrying incessantly about what the future might hold. Fortunately, though, it was all for naught. Although I did indeed lose the best boyfriend I ever had, what I found was much more exciting: the most incredible husband who ever walked the face of the Earth. Even better, some semblance of infatuation is still alive and well in our relationship. We now live a life I never thought possible.

Ruts in the Road

Daily living is, without a doubt, the most hectic business on the planet. We rush to the workplace day after day, solving one problem after another. There are meetings to attend, schedules to juggle, and complicated agendas to sort through.

It's a load too hefty for even the Fairy Godmother to handle, but that doesn't stop us. We just keep moving forward, trudging right through until everything is done. By the time we're through, exhaustion is a thing of the past. In fact, we're doing well to remember our own names.

Unfortunately, it doesn't stop there. On the way home we pick up the dry cleaning, handle personal errands, and tend to an assortment of other things that need our attention. We walk into a messy house to find overflowing laundry bins and a hungry family. Do we ignore it and relax? No. We just keep on pushing. We just keep on working. We just keep on rushing around until everything is nice and neat and in its proper place again. In fact, we get so caught up in what has to be done that we hardly have time to think. The only thing on our minds is crawling into bed—and the annoying alarm clock that will jolt us from sleep in just a few short hours.

This is where we get into trouble. With so much on our plates, real thinking goes by the wayside. We begin to do things methodically, routinely, and automatically. Life becomes boring. The fact that we're living it with the love of our lives really doesn't matter anymore. We view it as nothing more than some humdrum mess engineered by a team of puppeteers, all of whom insist that we dance to their personal tunes.

This is no way to live, especially not with the mate of your dreams. But how do you stop? How do you take back your life? More important, how do you get back to that place in your mind where love was the only thing that mattered?

Admittedly, it's a tricky business. It can be done, however, if you just set a few ground rules. The key here, though, is following through. Once you set the rules, you have to stick to them. You have to be tough. If you even think of pushing them aside, just remember why you picked up this book in the first place: to find the love of a lifetime–that person you couldn't live without and who could single-handedly leave you breathless, quivering, and begging for more. That alone should be enough to keep you on track.

Taking Control

Although you may find other ways to reclaim your life and bring you back in control, the rules that follow work well for everyone. Give them a shot and see what happens. If you find that other steps are necessary, don't hesitate to add them. The sooner you do, the sooner everything will fall back into place—and the sooner you'll be living the fairy-tale life you always dreamed of.

- ℅ **The 30-minute plan.** Quitting your job usually isn't an option, but how you use your time at home is up to you. Spend the first 30 minutes at home unwinding with your mate. Share the events of the day, both good and bad. Find something to laugh over. You'll both feel much better for it, and the rest of the evening will go much more smoothly.

- ℅ **Share the cooking.** No matter how you slice it, folks have to eat. Because everybody's hungry by the time they get home, it's not fair for one person to shoulder all the responsibility. A more reasonable solution is to share the cooking duties. Either take turns cooking dinner or cook together. (The latter can be a lot of fun, and can bring some humor to your evening.)

○ **Allocate one evening per week for errands.** Although things are bound to pop up now and then, you really don't have to run errands every day after work. Just jot down things as you think of them, then tend to the entire list on only one evening each week. Doing so will not only save your nerves and drive time, but will allow extra time at home.

○ **Clean the house once a week.** No one ever died from dust bunnies, suffered at the hands of a dirty carpet, or was ever swallowed whole by clutter. The point is that the house won't explode if it's not cleaned every single night. Plan, instead, to handle these chores on Sunday morning. That not only gives you Saturday to goof off, but it leaves Sunday afternoon free for quality time with your mate.

○ **Share the household duties.** Working together cuts cleaning time in half. In fact, if one of you scrubs floors while the other does the laundry or pays bills, you may just find some time for the important things—like spending time together. Although most of the chores can be handled separately, make an exception for making the bed. Doing this together is not only fun, but can be extremely sexy!

○ **Grocery shop together.** It's only natural for one or the other of you to have to run to the store for bread or milk, but plan time to do the bulk of the shopping together. It's a great way to get it done posthaste while having fun and spending time together.

Strict adherence to the guidelines just offered usually solves the problem. You find time to be together, to enjoy each other, and to rekindle that breathless, wondrous feeling that brought the two of you together. However, there may come a day when the guidelines themselves seem to cause a problem and require too much effort. And that's when most folks simply revert back to the old routine of rush and hurry. That's no way to live, and it certainly doesn't have to happen to you. All it takes is a firm decision to live your life, control where it goes, and reclaim your power. It's not that hard, especially if you perform the following spell.

Take-Back-Our-Lives Spell

<u>Materials list:</u>
  1 purple candle
  1 tsp. commanding incense
      (Alternatively, substitute 1/4 tsp. each
      powdered allspice, cinnamon, clove,
      and patchouli.)
  Vegetable oil
  Newspaper

On the full to new moon, gather the materials and head for the kitchen. Spread several sheets of newspaper on the counter and place the incense (or spices) on top. Anoint the candle with vegetable oil as you visualize the power you hold over your own life. Then roll the candle in the incense (take care to coat it well) and see yourself forcefully removing all the problems that usurp your time. Once they're all gone, chant:

We hold the power and we have the
    strength
To take back our lives and control them
    at length
As wick and wax burns—as the flame
    dances bright
We take our command and our loads we
    make light
We cast off all problems that creep, net,
    and snare
As well as new duties that promise to
    tear
Us away from each other as this life we
    claim
We cast them all out with no guilt and
    no shame
And as we take this stance on
    reclaiming this life
This spell culminates in removing all
    strife

Let the candle burn completely down, then bury
any wax remnants in the ground.

Crossed Wires

You've reclaimed your life and found quality time to
spend together. Even so, though, something's missing. Your
relationship seems anything but romantic. In fact, common
ground itself seems to have gone by the wayside. It's almost
as if the two of you, the lovers whose hearts once beat as
one, are now dancing separate steps to separate tunes. That
being so, there's no way you can dance together.

Or is there? Absolutely. You just have to understand a few things first.

To start with, men and women think differently, act differently, and have two separate chemical makeups. Simply put, they just aren't wired the same. It's a good thing, too, because if they handled everything in the same fashion, they wouldn't be drawn to each other in the first place.

The infatuation process, however, screws things up a bit. It causes a temporary sort of chemical imbalance in the brain. As a result, reality takes a back seat to fantasy. It's why we don't see obvious flaws. It's why we overlook things that we ordinarily wouldn't. In fact, it's wholly responsible for the process of falling in love.

Somewhere along the way, though, infatuation begins to fade. It's not that we aren't in love anymore or that the relationship is over; nothing could be further from the truth. It's just that the courting process is over, and because we *are* in love the brain no longer sees the infatuation mode as a necessary part of our lives. Things fall back into normalcy.

Of course, the heart doesn't understand this at all. It begins to question things—silly things that shouldn't be questioned to start with. Trouble starts to brew. Before we can stop ourselves, there we are: stirring the cauldron and creating a mess out of nothing. It's just another case of the utter chaos caused by the inability of the heart and mind to work together.

That's all well and fine. But what can we do to fix things? More importantly, how can we live happily ever after with our mates even when they seem to have misplaced their mystery and their sense of charm? It's simple. We just need to dispel a few myths.

Let's start with the thinking process. There is a physiological reason that men and women don't think the same way, and it has to do with minor anatomical differences. Here's how it works: During the thought process, one or more impulses travel up and down the spinal cord, then back to the brain. The thought is processed and becomes a part of the memory bank. This part of the process is the same for men and women.

The route that the impulses take to reach the brain and complete the thought process, however, is where things differ. The impulses bounce from four points in the male brain to complete the process, whereas they travel through six in the female brain. Although the number of points involved has nothing to do with which sex thinks more quickly, it has everything to do with the way that thoughts are processed. Because men basically think in a square, their thoughts tend to have an analytical edge. The circular pattern in women is softer and more emotional. This means that the very same thought is usually viewed by the sexes from completely different angles. So there's no way we can always expect our partners to totally grasp where we're coming from—at least, not without some digging and prodding and further conversation.

Although this may seem mind-boggling at first, it also helps to explain why men and women don't act alike. Because of the male angle, most men have an inherent need to protect and provide. They are natural warriors, hunters, and bread-winners. Most women, on the other hand, are born nurturers and caregivers. They can take on the troubles of the world, sort them out, and fix them all in the blink of an eye. Best of all, they manage to handle the whole thing with a soft touch and a healthy dose of tender loving care. This combination strikes a very good balance, indeed, because one provides what the other can't. Unfortunately, though, it can also cause a hell of a mess if we don't understand why we're different.

Let's say, for example, that the two of you find a badly injured animal on the side of the road. It's obvious that something should be done and you both want to help. One of you wants to care for the animal and do whatever it takes to heal its wounds. The other sees the damage and thinks that putting it out of its misery would be much kinder. Sparks fly. The fight of the century follows. Before all is said and done, not only are neither of you speaking to the other, but neither of you can possibly imagine what was so attractive about the other in the first place.

Of course, the best solution would have been to take the animal to the clinic and let the vet decide what to do, but things didn't even get that far. Because each of you were thinking and acting from different angles, stubbornness set in. Talking it over never entered the picture. One of you made a decision that didn't sit well with the other, and a horrible mess ensued, all because you both wanted to help.

To prevent this sort of thing from happening, you both need to understand the other's thought processes and subsequent actions. Then you need to think about what originally brought you together. Chances are, it was the differences. It was the fact that your partner provided something you needed (a necessary but lacking component such as strength, gentleness, or independent thinking) and managed to supply it in such a way that made you feel incredibly special.

You also need to decide if you really want to spend the rest of your life with someone who always thinks and reacts to every situation exactly as you do. More to the point, do you really want to wake up to a carbon copy of yourself on a daily basis?

Of course, you already know the answer. If any of those things were true, you wouldn't have been scouting out the perfect mate at all. In fact, you'd have been perfectly happy and more than satisfied just living alone.

Do yourself a favor. Don't just embrace your differences; be thankful for them. Even more importantly, learn to appreciate them. Those bits of diversity are exactly what brought you together in the first place. They are precisely the things that make you a good team. They comprise the individual components that make you whole and keep you dancing together, step by step, on solid ground, even when you think you can't.

If It's Not Broken...

"If it's not broken, don't fix it" was my Dad's favorite adage. He used it in all areas of his life and did his best to install it in ours. In fact, he said it so many times during the course of my childhood, I thought I might choke if I heard it once more. Once I was grown, though, I began to see its wisdom. Lucky for me, I've never forgotten it.

Unfortunately, the rest of the world seldom sees things that way, especially when it comes to intimate relationships. No matter how good things are, folks have some inherent need to make things better. They dream of flawlessness and perfection—an impeccable relationship draped in the folds of nirvana. Then they set out to make it happen. It doesn't matter that it won't. They just keep right on, pushing and prodding and trying to shape the relationship into what they think it should be: something that only exists in their dreams. In the final analysis, all they get for their troubles is a screwed-up mess that even the Ancients couldn't sort through. Worst of all, though, they usually wind up destroying the very attributes in their mates that were so wonderful to start with.

It begins innocently enough. Usually, there's just one little thing that needs improvement, one little thing that, if changed, would bring absolute perfection. Such was the case with me.

When my ex and I met, he was positively entranced by my sense of independence. There was nothing I couldn't plan, nothing I couldn't handle, and nothing that I couldn't see right through to the finish. Best of all, though, I took the initiative. I really didn't need supervision or outside help. I just made things happen.

Because he'd never encountered anyone quite like me, he was thrilled. I not only worked a 60-hour week, but I attended school functions, handled the finances, and managed all the home-related details with an efficiency he hadn't thought possible. Even better, I always had time for him. I seemingly ran everything by remote control, and he just couldn't believe his good luck.

Unfortunately, though, that sort of independence also breeds strength. And I was no exception to the rule. Even worse, I had opinions about everything. Some were important, so I voiced them. Those that weren't I kept to myself. Even so, the constant stream of discussions that he didn't feel were necessary began to get on his nerves. The strength, which he now viewed as sheer stubbornness, annoyed him. So he set about devising a plan to remove these items totally and irrevocably from our lives.

I won't bore you with all the details, but I will tell you this: He certainly didn't get what he bargained for. In trying to break my spirit and turn me into someone who I could never be, he screwed himself. I no longer provided him with a near-perfect life. (I couldn't have if I'd wanted to. I just didn't have that sort of stamina anymore.) I no longer juggled 50 things without dropping the ball. (How could I? My self-confidence was gone.) At the end of it all, there wasn't a lot of time left over for him. (I was much too tired to do anything but pull the covers up over my head.) He wasn't happy, I wasn't happy, and it was, for all practical purposes, the beginning of the end.

The point is twofold. First, only fools think they can ever really change someone else. More to the point, they should never try. Why? Because it never works out the way they envision. They may change them on the surface. They may even think they see results. But deep down inside whatever was still remains—waiting and watching and afraid to come out. And that breeds resentment—an emotion that eventually rears its ugly head and bites you in the butt.

Second, and perhaps more important, trying to initiate such a change (especially in the near-perfect partner) can ruin all semblance of happiness. That which was so attractive at the onslaught simply flies right out the window. All that's left is the monster you created, and there's nothing wondrous or attractive about that at all.

That said, I urge you to leave well enough alone. If it's not broken, don't fix it. Just enjoy what you have. Know that it's as perfect as it gets. And if things really start to get on your nerves, take a good hard look at why. You may find that the necessary changes don't really involve your partner at all. You may discover, instead, that they need to come from you.

Refurbishing the Heart/h

Now that we've gotten all that straightened out, it's time to get back to the infatuation phase. Granted, this may take some doing, but if you're going to live happily ever after, it's something you'll have to master again. After all, no one—

not even Prince Charming and Princess Perfect—can live in the same house day after day without getting bored, unless he or she is able to fall in love again on a regular basis. And reintroducing the infatuation factor to your lives is the only way to make it happen.

Of course, I could tell you to go back through the previous chapters and review all the tips about flirting, seduction, and romance, but that really won't do any good unless you're in the right mindset. You know the one: the spot where you feel absolutely wonderful and incredibly sick all at the same time, the place where first love spirits you off beyond all realm of common sense, and the point where you're so weak in the knees that you can hardly stand up. In order to get there, you have to look at each other with a fresh eye.

Walking down memory lane

One of the best ways to do this is to take a trip down memory lane. Remember all the things about your partner that used to make you smile, the things that used to make you laugh, and the way your heart used to leap from your chest every time he or she came into view.

Then recall some of your most memorable dates. Visualize them in detail. If you're the sentimental type (and most folks are, especially when caught up in the throes of new love) you probably have small mementos of some of the really special times, such as theater tickets, florist cards, and other souvenirs. Pull them out and pay close attention to the first thought that comes to your mind when you look at them. Chances are it won't be the actual event but something else, something much more important. What you'll recall is a valuable link in the chain of events that made you fall in love in the first place.

My first real date with my husband, for example, involved a St. Louis Cardinals game. I love baseball and am particularly fond of the Cardinals. Aside from that, it was the year of McGwire, and the seats were incredible. Those things on their own made it a very exciting date. It was also the hottest day of the year—the hottest day in 25 years, to be exact—and the heat index was such that newscasters everywhere were begging folks to stay indoors.

When I came across those ticket stubs a few days ago, though, those details weren't among my immediate thoughts. What I recalled, instead, was the funny face my husband made as he tried to drink that way-too-sweet lemonade. I remembered the hand-held walk through the park after the game, the green shade of the trees, and the cool respite of the park bench as we sat watching the barges go down river. Most of all, though, I remembered the way he looked at me as we chatted. It was as if no one else existed and as if the whole world had chosen that particular place in time to revolve solely around the two of us.

Now that you know how this works, grab some paper and jot down your thoughts. Work with each event separately. Don't worry if what you remember really has nothing to do with the exact details of the event itself. To be perfectly honest, I can't even remember who actually won that Cardinals game. That doesn't matter. What's important here are the first thoughts that pop into your head.

What if you didn't think to keep souvenirs? What then? Not to worry. Begin by jotting down the circumstances of every date you can remember sharing with your love and go on from there.

When you're finished (and this may take some time) go back and look at what you've written. Then make plans to re-create some of the events. Of course, you may not be able to duplicate them exactly, but with a little thought and effort, you can come pretty close. I can't, for example, duplicate our good fortune at being in the stands when Dale Earnhardt won the Talladega 500 in October of 1999. I can, however, rekindle that sort of excitement. I can even manage a reasonable facsimile of the day's events. That's all that's important. All you're trying to do here is re-create the portions that matter most, the ones closest to your heart, for those are the things that first infected you both with the mysteries of infatuation and the stirrings of new love.

How do I Love Thee?

Another way to conjure the spell of infatuation comes in the form of a small plastic box. It isn't very expensive, it's easy to use, and best of all, it's readily available at bookstores and stationery shops everywhere. This wonderful tool is none other than magnetic poetry.

If you're not familiar with this device, you're really missing out. It comes in different genres (love and romance, erotica, holiday, etc.) and is constructed from sheets of words that can be cut apart to create any message you want. (If you have trouble finding particular genres, try the magnetic poetry Web site at *www.magneticpoetry.com*.) Because they're magnetized, you can post the notes on any metal surface: the refrigerator, the range hood, or even the framework of the bathroom mirror.

What does this have to do with infatuation? Everything! For one thing, some people are too shy to say what they really want or how they really feel. No matter how hard they try, they simply can't force the words from their mouths. Other folks just don't express themselves well verbally. Because their thoughts flow more smoothly in written form, magnetic poetry is the perfect solution. Anyway you slice it, these little gems are dynamite when it comes to rekindling the fires of infatuation you felt at the beginning of your relationship.

I discovered magnetic poetry a few months ago as I was leaving a bookstore. My husband has a thing for refrigerator magnets, so magnetic poetry seemed like the perfect gift. I wasn't sure he'd use it, but that didn't matter. All I really cared about at the time was that he'd know I'd been thinking of him.

After they sat on top of the microwave for a week—uncut and unused—I decided to give it a whirl myself. I left a simple "I love you madly" on the fridge just as I left for a business trip. Fortunately, that was all it took. I came back home to provocative little messages everywhere, and the fun has yet to stop. In fact, we really look forward to the messaging, the search game it involves, and the romantic mood it evokes.

If this idea appeals to you but you're not sure how to get started, just grab your box of poetry and finish the sentence fragments provided here. Be warned, though: Once you get started, you may never want to stop!

Message ideas

- ◌ I would trudge through puppy drool to _____ .
- ◌ I want to lick your _____ .
- ◌ I want to _____ until your toes curl.
- ◌ You make my heart _____ .
- ◌ Your love is like _____ .
- ◌ I am delirious over _____ .
- ◌ The very thought of your luscious _____
  makes me want to _____ .

Now that you've gotten the hang of it, spend some time constructing your own messages. Be sappy, be provocative, or just be downright graphic. The choice is yours. Worst case scenario? Your hearts will race. You'll feel sick. You'll feel fabulous. You'll feel it all at the same time. In this case, though, it's nothing to worry about. You're just falling in love with each other again—and that's exactly what you set out to accomplish in the first place.

Infatuation Spell

Because infatuation is infectious, the least amount of effort normally brings it back into play. If you've let things slip for a while, though, it may need some prodding, just a little something to help it along. And that's where this spell comes in.

Materials list:

> 2 pink candles
> Vanilla oil
> Metal pan or other fireproof dish
> Long-handled grill lighter (A cigarette
>   lighter or fireplace matches work in a
>   pinch.)
> Pen or pencil

Wait for a Friday when the moon is waxing or full. Use the pen or pencil to inscribe your name on one candle and your mate's on the other. Anoint the candles and place them side by side in the pan with the names facing toward you. Run the flame of the lighter along the inner sides of the candles to melt some of the wax and quickly push them together. (The candles should now be stuck to each other as one.)

Using the pencil, and being careful not to dislodge the candles, draw a half-heart around one name and a half-heart around the other. (When facing the candles, this will appear as if one heart encases both names.)

Light the wicks and visualize how things were for the two of you at the beginning of the relationship and how you felt when you saw each other. Remember how your hearts nearly leapt from your chests. Then bring that feeling into present day. See it happening all over again. Feel the feeling—only with more strength and power than it ever held before—and chant:

> Infatuation come to play
> Come at once and come to stay
> Weave your magic strong and well
> Enchant us with your ancient spell
> So that we feel what we once felt
> As if our very hearts would melt
> When the other passed in view
> Do now what I ask of you

Let the candles burn down completely. Toss any leftover wax into a running body of water.

Kindling the Fire

So, you're infatuated again. Your whole world seems a little off-kilter. What's more, it's taken on that sweet, sappy, romantic glow again—the one that signals love, provides a new attitude, and makes you think that nothing is impossible. Of course, you want to keep it that way.

The good news is that it doesn't have to fade. Its fragrance can surround you for the rest of your lives. Just as a rose does, though, it needs some care. A bit of special tending to keep it healthy, alive, and blooming. Otherwise, it will simply shrivel and die—and that's the last thing you want to see happen.

Fortunately, there is a simple solution. Just set aside one day each month and use it solely to tend your romance and nurture your love. Use it to enjoy each other. It isn't much to ask. After all, it's only 12 days a year, and the benefits reaped will far outweigh the effort.

It's a great idea, but what if it isn't plausible? What if you have children to tend or your schedule just won't allow it? If these problems apply to you, maybe a few minutes of remembrance are in order. Just go back to the time when finding the love of your life was all that mattered. Think about all the trouble you endured to find it. Remember how you planned and created. Now that you've gotten exactly what you dreamed of, stop and ask yourself this question: Are you willing to simply let it slip through your fingers permanently and irrevocably? I don't think so.

Tending to children is the easy part. Just pick up the phone and call a babysitter. If that's not an option, arrange a sleepover for them with friends with a promise to reciprocate later. Don't worry that the kids will resent it or that you're a bad parent. They'll have such a good time they won't want to come home.

Handling scheduling problems may take a little more effort, but they can be sorted through by way of a wall calendar. Just add your agendas to the appropriate days and see when you're both available. Circle the day in red and refuse to let anything interfere, especially guilt complexes tossed in by tenacious friends or employers. Simply say that you have a previous engagement and let it go at that.

When the scheduled day arrives, you'll want to make sure that nothing interferes with your privacy, and the last thing you'll want to worry about is cooking dinner. With that in mind, take a little initiative. Call your favorite restaurant and arrange to pick up some take-out in advance. Failing that, prepare a meal the night before to reheat.

If children are involved, tell their temporary caregivers that you may not be able to be reached by phone until the next day. Then offer a notarized note giving them the authority to make surgical decisions for your kids should they be necessary. (Don't worry. Nothing will happen. It's just the responsible way to cover all bases.) Then turn off the ringer and turn down the volume on the answering machine. (That way you'll know if there's a true emergency.) The whole idea, after all, is to spend some time enjoying each other, and whoever is calling can wait.

You'll also want to keep neighbors and friends at bay, especially if they're the type who drop in at a moment's notice. Of course, you could always refuse to answer the door. But a better plan involves a preventative measure: Just leave a note on the door to shoo folks away. It doesn't have to be anything fancy. Simply explain that you love them, but this is your time—time that you intend to spend together, devoid of all interruptions. (If your friends are the persistent type, you may want to add *"Go away. This means you."*)

With all of that taken care of, there's nothing left for you to do but enjoy each other. Snuggle, cuddle, and revel in the glowing warmth of love and romance. If you are ready to turn up the heat a bit, read on. You'll find ways to take each other to new heights—heights where only the voracious flames of passion have nerve enough to dance wild and free.

Fanning the Flames

Although the tips on dressing for love in Chapter 3 definitely heighten the initial stages of attraction, something else is in order when you reach this stage of the romantic game: something sexy, something spicy, something even a little bit naughty. That something, of course, has to do with knowing exactly how to *undress* for love.

Undressing for love is important because it provides the spark that keeps relationships going despite all outside annoyances and aggravations. It kindles the fire and warms the heart. Above all, it brews the fondest memories life has to offer. It's those memories that are truly important. Without them, we wouldn't find any reason to go to work every day, scrub the toilet, or cook a meal. Without them, there simply wouldn't be any impetus to keep going home to the same person day after day. Because of them, though, we can manage anything that life dishes out. Simply put, those memories give us hope.

Unfortunately, there is no instant formula for undressing. In fact, it's solely dependent on what pushes your mate's sexual buttons. For some folks, it's garter belts and fishnet stockings. For others, it's silk boxers or thongs. It's a simple matter of what, in effect, turns him or her on. And if you've been doing your homework, you should already have this information.

But what if you don't? What if you've somehow managed to keep the relationship going without having the slightest clue? Not to worry. There are lots of ways to get this information. Unless you're willing to just come right out and ask (which is doubtful, because you haven't already) just go back to what sort of lover you're living with and gear your plans specifically to his or her type. (For further information on types, see the section on love matches in Chapter 3.) The following tips will get you started.

- ℬ **Lovers of Sight.** Because these mates absolutely revel in naughty visuals, you'll want to don the steamiest lingerie possible. Leather and lace are good bets, as are garter belts and thongs. (Don't smirk, guys. Thongs on men can be extremely titillating, too!) If you don't have a lingerie shop or adult bookstore in your neighborhood, don't worry. Just go the mail-order route or make your purchases via the Internet. Then toss a romantic movie into the VCR (or really turn up the heat with a triple-X video). Your mate will be salivating before you know it!

- ℬ **Lovers of Sound.** Modes of undress can be a bit trickier with these mates, because they don't always respond to the things that our society normally promotes as sexy. That being the case, it's a good idea to turn off the phone and set the mood with some provocative music. Whatever you like is fine, as long as the beat and the lyrics are hot and stimulating. Once your mate's in the mood, top things off with a little pillow talk. If you're the shy type, start out slowly and become more graphic as you get the hang of it. Remember: Always use his or her name while you're talking. You may not even make it to the bedroom!

- ℬ **Lovers of Emotion.** When it comes to pleasing these mates, it's hard to beat the tactile sensuality of silk or satin gowns, pajamas, and bedding. Because lovers of emotion also love the feel of smooth skin, though, don't skimp on the body lotion. Undress each other slowly and deliberately, caressing any newly exposed skin. Then hold each other and dance naked in your living room to slow, romantic music. Afterward, lead your partner to the bedroom—and the bed that you've so sumptuously strewn with rose petals. It's guaranteed to be a night that you'll never forget!

Sexual Spice

Although the aforementioned tips apply to specific types of mates, there are literally tons of other ideas that appeal to all lovers. Used in combination, they can leave your partner weak in the knees, quivering with delight, and begging for more. In fact, they can do more for your relationship than all the "I love you's" in the world. For your convenience, some of the most effective are listed here. Don't stop there, though. Engage your imagination and act on your fantasies. You may just come up with something so hot, so sexy, and so erotically tantalizing that it will rekindle the fires of your love into a steamy dance of flaming passion, the likes of which you've never before experienced.

CR **Draw your love a bath.** Not just any bath, mind you, but a royal one. Include bath oil or salts in a sensuous scent and scatter the surface of the water with rose petals. Place an array of candles on the bathroom counter, add some incense, and place a glass of wine within reaching distance of the tub. Light the candles and incense and turn out the lights. Then lead your love into the bathroom and slowly undress him or her. Bathe your partner with loving caresses, and dry with a large, fluffy towel before leading the way to bed. (For extra luxury, warm the towel in the dryer first.)

☙ **Dance for your love.** There is nothing more sensual than erotic dance, especially when it's being performed specifically for you by someone you adore. Start out by donning an oversized shirt and putting on some sultry, sexy music. Then move your hips and dance, using the shirttails as a flirting device. Flip them up. Flip them down. Keeping your eyes locked on your love, unfasten the shirt one button at a time, slowly and deliberately. Move in such a way that your partner knows that he or she arouses you like no other person on the planet and that the only thing on your mind is the pleasure that's bound to follow.

☙ **Make love somewhere other than the bedroom.** Because there's something forbidden about sex in other rooms, this can prove to be very arousing. Try the living room, the dining room, the hall, or the kitchen. If you're feeling especially daring (and tend to fantasize about being "caught") quickies in an elevator, a storage room, or an airplane bathroom can be exhilarating, too.

☙ **Make love in the middle of the day.** Somewhere along the line, we get the idea that the pleasures of love-making should always be reserved for the shadowy darkness of the night. Nothing, however, is further from the truth, and if you subscribe to that fallacy, you're really missing out. Once you enjoy the sensual pleasures of bare skin exposed to daylight, you may never again have sex in the dark!

ભ **Rent a hotel room.** This can be especially exciting if you reserve the room without telling your mate. Just pack up whatever you'll need for the night and leave the room key for your mate with a note requesting his or her presence. Wait for your love in the hotel room dressed in nothing but a tie or a bow around your neck.

ભ **Act out your fantasies.** There's nothing quite like fantasy to pump up your sex life or gain some insight into your partner. Because you trust your partner and know that he or she would never harm you, even the wildest fantasies are fair game. Absolutely anything can be simulated to perfection. You just have to give it a little thought and make a few plans.

What if you're still not sure about any of this? There's nothing worse, after all, than going to tons of trouble if you've still got a nagging feeling that your efforts may not work. If that's the case with you, then help is on the way. Just whip up some of the magical goodies that follow. They're guaranteed to whisk away your inhibitions as well as your partner's.

Lusty sheet scent

1 tsp. cinnamon
1 tsp. ginger
1 drop vanilla oil
2 drops musk oil
1 clean sock

Place the first four ingredients inside the sock and knot the end securely to provide a pouch. Toss it in the dryer with your bedding and chant:

> Herbs and oils, increase desire
> Bring sexual tension hot as fire
> So when these sheets are back to bed
> No other thoughts run through the head

Place the dried, scented sheets on the bed. The results will amaze you!

Flames of Desire Incense

8 dried red rose buds
1 tsp. cinnamon
1 tsp. allspice
1/2 tsp. ginger
1/4 tsp. chili powder

Place all ingredients in a blender and mix on high for a minute or two to reduce the mixture to powder. Empty the powder into a jar. Holding the jar in both hands, say:

> Spice of love, like burning fire
> Kindle in us hot desire
> 'Til we are one instead of two
> Do now what I ask of you

Burn the mixture on a charcoal block or simmer it in an electric potpourri pot wherever you plan to make love.

Edible lust lotion

1 oz. melted cocoa butter
1 T. coconut oil
1/4 c. corn syrup
1/2 tsp. flavoring extract of your choice (optional)

Combine the ingredients in a blender on high speed for a few minutes. As they blend, say:

For hottest sex and yummy taste
You powers are forever laced
Together to complete this task
I conjure you to what I ask

Apply this lotion wherever you think it might feel or taste good. Use your imagination.

All-night-long massage oil

1 oz. almond, jojoba, or grape seed oil
1 drop cinnamon oil
2 drops vanilla oil
2 drops musk oil
1 pinch amber

Combine the ingredients and swirl to blend. During the blending process, chant:

All night long is what I ask
Combine and blend to suit the task
Fears be gone, so stamina rules
Become a lust-provoking tool

Massage your partner with the oil to release inhibitions and increase sexual stamina.

Dying Embers

No matter how deeply two people love each other—or how infected with infatuation they may be—it sometimes happens that sex drives just don't cooperate. One partner needs more; the other needs less. When that's the case, all sorts of problems can take shape. Insecurities surface and tensions abound.

Left untended, the least little thing (a look, a comment, or a simple tilt of the head) can birth a monster so fiercely powerful that even the Fairy Godmother herself couldn't whisk it away.

Fortunately, this monster doesn't have to destroy your lives. In fact, he doesn't even have to be born. You can stop him in his tracks before he draws his first breath. All it takes is a healthy dose of understanding and some strong, open lines of communication. It's an easy enough solution, and you don't even have to be a Fairy Godperson to meet with success.

Sadly enough, though, most folks simply refuse to talk about this sort of thing. It's embarrassing to them. They don't want to push the envelope, put their partner on the defensive, or cause hurt feelings. So instead, they just sit there, silent and reclusive, worrying and wondering and breeding scores of personal insecurities that they could do well without.

Because most couples in love don't have a problem with understanding, though, we'll start with that. There are literally dozens of reasons why your partner's sex drive may not meet yours. Mental exhaustion or physical exertion can be key factors, especially if they're not balanced with an equal amount of good old-fashioned relaxation. Daily worries or performance anxieties (even if unfounded) could come into play. Something as simple as a side effect from a prescription medication could be an issue. At any rate, you need to understand that you're probably not at all responsible for the problem. More than likely, it's something so minute, so inconspicuous, and so trivial that you never even gave it a second thought.

Then, no matter how uncomfortable you are with the situation, gently bring it up for discussion. Your partner won't shy away if you initiate the conversation lovingly. In fact, he or she will embrace the opportunity to discuss things if given half a chance. It's just a matter of having the courage to open the door. So go ahead and take the first step. You'll both feel better for it.

Because these are sensitive issues to everyone concerned, they often require special handling. For that reason, here are some suggestions for dealing with some of the most common problems. Just remember to tender them all with patience and understanding. Things will be back to normal before you know it.

- CS **Exhaustion.** This is, undoubtedly, the most common cause of low libido and sexual dysfunction. Fortunately, it's also the easiest to cure. The answer? Rest, relaxation, and lots of sleep. Just give your partner a few days and see what happens. With sufficient rest, he or she won't be able to leave you alone.

- CS **Previously undisclosed feelings and emotions.** These sorts of issues usually stem from the formation of emotional buttons and related fears. The best way to handle them is to stay calm, supportive, and attentive. Allow your partner to voice all of his or her insecurities. Then remind him or her that this is a new day, that all those concerns are yesterday's news, and that from this day forward, you'll do everything in your power to keep them at bay. Mean it and take steps toward allaying any further fears.

- CS **Unmet sexual needs.** Sometimes people crave something sexually that they don't have the nerve to request. Why? Because they are afraid that their partner will think there's something wrong with them. In this case, just lay any fears to rest and find out what it is. Chances are, it's no big deal and you'll be more than willing to comply. If, however, you find the request distasteful, see what you can do about striking a compromise. A little effort in this direction can rectify things immediately.

❧ **Performance anxiety.** Even when couples have been together for a while, performance anxieties can resurface. This is nobody's fault; it's just a strange phenomenon that occasionally occurs. If that's the case, simply remove any undue pressures to perform. Let your partner know that you enjoy snuggling and cuddling immensely and that not every close encounter needs to result in sex.

❧ **Unknown cause.** It's also possible that your partner doesn't have any idea why his or her sex drive isn't behaving properly. If that's the case, don't worry. Just make an appointment for your partner to see the doctor. It could be that a current prescription medication is the culprit. It could also be that he or she is a candidate for one of the many safe sexual enhancement drugs currently on the market.

Fires of Desire Spell

Once you've brought things out into the open and discussed them at length, you'll both feel better. Tensions will dissipate. Your life—along with wonderful, hot, passionate love-making—will quickly resume. But don't stop there: Use the following spell as a safeguard. It's guaranteed to keep this sort of thing from happening again, and it provides an insurance policy you'll want to keep on hand.

Materials list:

- 1 small potted cyclamen plant (Substitute a rosemary or parsley plant if you prefer.)
- 1 plant saucer to fit the size of the pot
- 1 small relationship crystal (Substitute a piece of carnelian or sunstone if you prefer.)
- 2 fertilizer sticks
- 1 permanent marking pen
- 1 red candle
- Pen or pencil
- Water

Begin by gathering your materials on a Sunday, Thursday, or Friday during the waxing moon. Using the pen or pencil, inscribe the candle with a circle. Draw a cross at the very top of the circle boundary so that the vertical line touches the inscribed curvature. Draw an arrow in the same way at the bottom of the circle. Light the candle and say:

> By sign of male and female each
> This flame shall bring within our reach
> A love with hot and lusty sex
> In which the two of us shall flex
> Entwined together—just we two
> By flame, Desire, I conjure you

Using the permanent marking pen, draw the same symbol on the front of the plant's pot and say:

By signs of woman and of male
I enchant this living plant and pail
And as it grows, so will our lust
For each other as it must
Until libidos step in time
And join together in the rhyme
Of sex and love and fantasy
As I will, so mote it be

Holding the two fertilizer sticks together as one, plunge them into the soil. Set the plant into the saucer and fill it with water. Leave the pot in front of the candle until the wick burns out.

Put the plant in the bedroom in a sunny spot and say:

Little plant so filled with lust
Do now what you know you must
Fan the flames and bright the fire
Of hottest sex and true desire
Bring back the passion we once knew
Do now what I ask of you

Fill the saucer with water whenever the soil is dry to the touch.

Grapevine Lust Charm

As long as you're performing lust magic, it's a good idea to make this charm. Hung on the bedroom wall or over the bed, it acts as an ongoing booster to keep sex drives on an even keel. Make it on the same day you perform the spell and you'll be well on the way to sensual delight!

Materials list:

- 1 round grapevine wreath in your choice of size (readily available at arts and crafts stores)
- 1 box whole cloves
- 6 tsp. cinnamon
- 1 tsp. ginger
- 1/4-yard red fabric (Cotton velveteen, satin, and calico prints are good choices)
- 1 yard red ribbon
- Needle and thread
- Scissors
- Pins
- Paper
- Pen or pencil
- Iron
- Polyester fiberfill (approx. a handful)
- Red silk flowers (optional)

Start by drawing a heart on the paper. (You'll want this to be a bit smaller than the inner circumference of the wreath.) Cut out the heart, then fold the fabric in half, right sides together. Pin the heart on top of the fabric and cut it out. Starting at the point of the heart on the left-hand side, stitch the figure together, leaving an opening on the lower right-hand side. Turn the heart inside out and press.

Fill the inner edges of the heart with fiberfill. Draw the figure described in the Fires of Desire Spell earlier in this chapter on a small piece of paper and write your names in the circle. Fold it in half, insert it into the heart, and say:

Entwined we are, thee and me
For as long as we shall want to be
Entwined in lust, entwined in love
Entwined as Moon and Sky above

Add the cloves, and say:

Little cloves of sex and lust
Manifest in both of us
Rawest sensual desire
Kindle now this lusty fire

Add the cinnamon and say:

Spicy herb of loving care
Tender now this lusty fare
So that we are true in love
Like Sun and Moon which shine above

Finally, add the ginger and say:

Ginger of the spicy fire
Add your flame to our desire
Make it grow and make it strong
So it lasts our whole love long

Finish filling the heart with fiberfill, then slipstitch
the opening shut. Fold the ribbon in half and sew the
fold to the upper back of the heart. Tie the heart to
the top of the wreath so that it swings freely in the
inner perimeter. Decorate the wreath with flowers if
you like.

When the wreath is to your liking, hang it on the
wall or over the bed and say:

Protect our lust—protect our love
Protect our romance from above
Do now what I ask of thee
As I will, so mote it be

Chapter Six

Happily Ever After

Everything you've read thus far has been perfectly designed toward the happy ending. It's all good advice, and, used as directed, happily ever after is exactly what you're headed for. There are a few more things you need to know, though—especially if you want to weave the love of a lifetime, that timeless sort of forever love that none of us can live without.

The gems that follow are mundane in nature. They have to do with remembrance, with celebration, and with commemoration. In short, they have to do with honoring particular dates that are important to each other. Forget them once, and all the hard work you've done will come crashing down around you. The rest of your life will be *anything* but happy.

The same is true if you don't celebrate them properly. These occasions (birthdays, anniversaries, Valentine's Day, the winter holidays, and so forth) are a big deal, and they call for major festivities and an obscene amount of attention. In these cases, a simple "I forgot" or "I didn't know what to get you" positively will not do.

This chapter is designed to help you handle these special occasions as only a real Prince Charming or Princess Perfect can. So pay close attention, follow the instructions, and then embellish them with frills and flourishes. Once you do, you'll never have to worry about your relationship coming apart at the seams. In fact, it will never provide you with anything but happiness.

The Birthday Bash

There is no such thing as overdoing this celebration, because no matter what your partner says, you're expected to make a fuss. That's because birthdays are a really big deal. It's the time we celebrate the reason that someone lives and breathes. If not for this day, we wouldn't have the pleasure to know them, to love them, or to share our lives with them. It's more than just a celebration of their very existence, though: It's also a day to celebrate all that they mean to us.

For these reasons, a major celebration is in order. That means going to an exorbitant amount of trouble. This may involve a surprise party, an elegant candlelit dinner, or maybe a night on the town with all the bells and whistles. If your mate seems happier with quiet celebrations, you might even opt for a romantic picnic or a sensual evening at home.

Whatever you decide, though, make sure that the festivities are geared solely toward your mate's happiness. This, after all, is your mate's day, and, for today, the things that bring a smile to his or her face are all that truly matter. Toss out any ideas about your own wants and wishes. But what if your mate wants to go somewhere that doesn't trip your trigger? Even worse, what if the plans include taking in some activity that isn't high on your priority list of fun things to do? Just relax and get with the program. It won't wound you permanently. It won't scar you for life. In fact, I can nearly guarantee that you'll live to see tomorrow.

Just remember that it's only one day out of 365. Besides, you'll have your turn, too, and on that day you can do exactly as you please.

The 10-Foot Pole Department

It's time to think about a birthday gift, which needs to be something special, unique, and designed with no one but your mate in mind. My father learned this the hard way when he lost all control of common sense and gave my mother a rifle for her birthday. It wasn't that he didn't know better; he did. Because Mama went hunting with him occasionally, he found a way to justify his actions. And for some unknown reason, he truly thought he could get away with it.

Of course, things didn't work out as he'd planned. Mama was just more than a little upset. She was peel-me-off-the-ceiling mad. When her anger subsided (and it eventually did) things went from bad to worse. She was hurt and offended. She collapsed into a pool of tears and just sat there for several hours. Fortunately for Daddy, it was something he never forgot.

Keeping that story in mind, always select birthday presents with the utmost care. Remember that this day is not about you. It's about your mate. Your selection should not only be something personal, but something that your mate would not ordinarily buy for him- or herself. In short, it should be something that your mate wants, *not* something that your mate needs.

Deciding on something appropriate can be exasperating to say the least. Thankfully, though, there is a relatively simple solution. Just find out what your mate would like. Of course, we usually don't think of handling things in this manner. Why? Because for some unknown reason, we believe that birthday gifts should always be a surprise. It's just one more fallacy that we insist on perpetuating, a myth with no basis in fact and a delusion that can breed serious trouble. For that reason, don't be afraid to ask some direct questions. If you still want to add an element of surprise, just ask a close friend instead. You'll be able to gain some insight into not only what might be appropriate but into what it will take to bring this day to the top of life's most memorable events.

If you still insist on surprising your mate (and most folks do) know that gift selection can be a tricky business at best. That's because individual tastes vary, and no one likes the same things. There are certain areas to avoid, however, and knowing what they are can be a tremendous help to all involved. That being the case, shy away from the areas that follow—unless there is a specific request for these items. You'll be glad you did.

- ⚜ **Household items.** These include kitchen gadgets, cookware, appliances, vacuum cleaners, towels, sheets, and so forth. You're not going to get the reaction you expected if your gift implies that your mate should do more work around the house.

- ⚜ **Tools.** Drills, saws, electric screwdrivers, work benches, gardening tools, and so forth are also taboo. As with household items, they give the impression that somehow, your partner isn't paying enough attention to home and garden needs.

- ⚜ **Undergarments.** Socks, underwear, robes, and slinky lingerie fall into this category. Although specialty underwear and lingerie might be appropriate for Valentine's Day or your anniversary, it simply will not work for a birthday. Besides, your mate can easily purchase these items without your input.

℘ **Sporting goods.** Sporting goods often make fabulous holiday gifts for the sports enthusiast, but birthdays call for something a little more luxurious. For that reason, shy away from camping/hunting equipment, ski gear, and related clothing.

℘ **Automobile accessories.** Slipcovers, steering-wheel covers, air fresheners, and other related gadgetry aren't luxury items; they're necessary equipment. That being the case, save them for your holiday list.

℘ **Office accessories.** This includes pen and pencil sets, desk sets, day planners, and so forth. The only exceptions to the rule are laptop and desktop computers and expensive computer peripherals.

℘ **Pets.** Although the thought of surprising your mate with a cuddly puppy or kitten may be charming, this is the absolute no-no when it comes to gift-giving. Pets are living creatures, they consume tons of time, and they lose their charm just as soon as they piddle on the floor. If you mate wants a pet, discuss it and pick one out together. But *never* give one as a gift.

Great Gift Ideas

Even though you know your love better than anyone else on the planet, some partners are just difficult to buy for. If that's the case with yours, don't despair. Just try some of the gift ideas offered here. They're geared toward specific partner types and may provide some insight into making this day a very happy one, indeed.

‹3 **Lovers of sight.** Movies, video games, limited edition prints, restored photographs, and paintings are always a good bet for this mate. Better yet, have a calendar made from photographs of the two of you. For a real treat, try tickets to an art show, a play, a baseball game, or some other event designed to tickle his or her fancy. Don't forget the flowers; lovers of sight absolutely adore them.

‹3 **Lovers of sound.** Just think audio when working on this gift list. Some great ideas include tickets to a concert, television taping, lecture series, or favorite stand-up act. Clocks (especially those with audible ticks), desktop water fountains, and wind chimes work well, too. If you're in a real pinch and don't have much time to shop, purchase a complete CD collection of your mate's favorite recording artist. It's a perfect gift that will lend hours of pure pleasure.

‹3 **Lovers of emotion.** Pampering and luxury are key words here, so anything that feels good automatically makes the perfect gift. Try clothing items in silk or cashmere or briefcases or handbags made of smooth, supple leather. A gift certificate for a therapeutic massage or an all-expenses-paid day at the spa are good bets as well. Do you want to really pamper your mate? Get up early and serve breakfast in bed. The day will be memorable indeed, and you'll reap the benefits!

Perfection Personified

If none of these ideas appeal to you, there is one gift that's always appropriate. That gift, of course, is jewelry. Although we normally think of women when it comes to jewelry, don't fool yourself. Men like it, too. There's nothing more luxurious than the rich feel of precious metals against the skin. In fact, it can turn any day into a real event.

When purchasing jewelry for your love, there are a few things you need to know. First, don't scrimp. This isn't a junior-high crush you're buying for; it's the love of your life. Keeping that in mind, pass on the costume jewelry. In this case, only sterling silver, gold, or platinum will do.

You also need to know what type of jewelry your mate likes. Some people may go in for pieces with a spiritual or New Age theme, and others may lean toward something more traditional. Personal style figures in here, too, so you will have to decide whether to shop for something dainty and old-fashioned or bold and contemporary. If you're in doubt, it's a good idea to check your mate's jewelry box. That will give you some insight into tailoring your purchase specifically toward his or her tastes.

One final word of advice for the guys here, especially those who are planning to buy a ring: There's nothing worse than presenting your love with something stunning that doesn't fit. The jeweler will be more than happy to resize the piece, but this process often takes up to two weeks. In the meantime, though, your love won't be able to wear it and could wind up very unhappy. For that reason, I urge you to check your mate's shoe size. Why? Because more than 95 percent of the time, her shoe size matches the size of her ring finger. And having this information at hand will save you tons of trouble in the long run.

Valentine's Day

Valentine's Day is observed all over the world as a celebration of romance. Letting this occasion pass by without some sort of acknowledgment is just asking for trouble. In fact, not doing enough could land you so far in the doghouse that you'll never again see the light of day.

The way couples celebrate this day varies, though. Some are perfectly happy with a card exchange. Others expect flowers and candy. Still others expect some sort of gift. It's all a matter of what they're used to.

This could present a problem if you're celebrating this holiday with your love for the first time. For one thing, you don't want to outdo your love. If one of you buys a diamond and the other only picks up a card, neither of you will be very happy. At the same time, you won't want to "underdo" it. You'll just wind up feeling like a cheapskate, and that's no way to celebrate the romance of the century.

My husband and I agreed to only exchange cards the first year. We'd just moved, we were trying to get things straightened out, and our work schedules were such that even managing to be together on Valentine's Day was quite a feat. I fixed a scrumptious meal, and we spent the evening cuddled up on the couch. It was wonderfully romantic.

The next year was a little different, though. He went to an exorbitant amount of trouble to make sure that it was an incredibly special day. Fortunately, a friend tipped me off in plenty of time. Had it not been for her concern, I might have just given him a card and wound up feeling like a complete idiot when I unwrapped a ruby and diamond pendant. For this reason, it's a good idea to discuss plans with your mate several weeks before the big day. You don't have to give away any surprises, but you'll both know what's expected and still have time to comply.

Great Gift Ideas

Although this holiday can be expensive, there are tons of ways to celebrate without dipping into your rent money. First, find the most romantic card available. Then use the following tips. They're all great ideas and are guaranteed to keep you out of the doghouse for a long time to come.

- ભ **Send flowers.** If you're looking for something other than the standard dozen roses, though, order a plant or a balloon bouquet instead. Talk to the florist early. If you don't place your order by the first week of February, you may wind up empty-handed.

- ભ **Go out to dinner.** Along with flowers, this is a Valentine's standard. Not just any restaurant will do, though. You'll want to pick one with just the right atmosphere. Something with candlelight, soft music, and cozy tables for two. Take care to make reservations early. Tables at good restaurants go really fast this time of year.

- ભ **Give lingerie.** Because there's a big difference between sexy and trashy, you'll want to be careful here. Remember that this day is about romance, and you'll want any purchases to reflect that. It's best to err on the side of elegance, so the rule of thumb is to stay away from nylon. Try silk or satin gowns, teddies, and pajamas for women, and silk or satin boxers, pajamas, or robes for men. Go to the trouble to get the right size. (Your mate won't feel very romantic if those delectable wrappings contain something that won't even fit his or her big toe!) If you're in doubt, it's okay to cheat: Check your mate's underwear or lingerie drawer.

✃ **Give gifts of sterling silver.** Because silver is the metal of the moon (and the moon affects human emotion) gifts of sterling silver are perfect for this occasion.

✃ **Heart-shaped charms,** pendants, and lockets are good bets for women. Paper weights, cigarette lighters, money clips, pocket watches, and ID bracelets are more suitable for men. If you want to add a really special touch, have the piece engraved with a romantic message.

✃ **Give candy.** This one isn't much trouble at all. In fact, you'll find heart-shaped boxes of chocolates in every store imaginable. If you want to go the extra distance for a really warm reception, though, opt for a box of Godiva truffles. Failing that, present your love with a florist's box filled with candy kiss rosebuds. (See the instructions that follow to make these.) It will provide a Valentine's Day that neither of you will ever forget!

Long-Stemmed Chocolate-Kiss Roses

I gave these little goodies to my husband as part of his Valentine's gift last year, and they were a huge hit. He was so entranced with them, in fact, that he showed them off to everyone on the construction site! These definitely aren't a stand-alone gift, but they make a great addition to any romantic trappings you may have in mind. Best of all, they're quick, easy, and inexpensive to make.

Materials list:

  1 bag chocolate kisses in red foil
     wrappers
  1 roll green florist tape
  1 florist box
  2 yards red florist ribbon
  Several packages silk rose leaves
  12 12-inch lengths heavy green florist
     wire
  4 sheets of green tissue paper
  Plastic wrap
  Wire cutters

Wrap two candy kisses (flat sides together) in a small piece of plastic wrap. Twist the plastic to secure. Insert a length of wire through the twisted plastic and into the tip of the candy (the point of one of the kisses). Then, holding the twisted plastic against the wire, wrap securely with florist tape to cover. Continue wrapping down the wire, adding rose leaves as you work. Cut to size with the wire cutters.

Tie the rosebuds together with the ribbon, finishing with a bow. Line the florist box with green tissue and place the rose buds inside. Add a deliciously romantic note and send by courier. Then sit back, relax, and wait for the phone to ring!

Engaging Your Love

If you've had marriage on the brain and just haven't had the nerve to propose, Valentine's Day provides the perfect setting. It is, after all, the most romantic day of the year, so the chances of engaging your love for a lifetime of sharing and commitment are better than ever. Besides, a marriage proposal delivered on Valentine's Day will bring romantic memories for the rest of your lives.

Keeping that in mind, though, you need to go to a little trouble with your proposal. This means that a simple "I think we ought to get married. What do you think?" may not provide the results you expected. A proposal on this day calls for a few flourishes, a few embellishments, something a little out of the ordinary—in other words, something that your love will never forget.

The traditional proposal calls for a down-on-one-knee self-effacing speech, but you may not be a traditional sort of person. There are lots of imaginative ways to handle this feat and still make it memorable. Because you'll also want to avoid any mishaps, though, it's a good idea to avoid the following:

- **A ring mixed into food or drink.** Even though this may seem romantic, it's an absolute no-no when it comes to the marriage proposal. Romance will fade quickly if your love chips a tooth or, even worse, swallows the ring and has to be rushed to the hospital for medical attention.

- **An ad to your love in the personals.** Here's another idea that may seem romantic at first. What if your love doesn't see it, though? You'll be waiting around for an answer that won't ever come. It's a problem just waiting to happen and one you certainly don't need.

- **A telephone or e-mail proposal.** This is definitely the coward's way out. I certainly wouldn't marry anyone who didn't have the courage to propose face-to-face. I doubt that you would, either.

Now that we've gotten those out of the way, there are any number of ways to pop the question both elegantly and memorably. You might propose during a moonlit walk. (The park or the beach can make a really romantic backdrops for this.) Another good idea is to propose with a toast to your love while on a wine and cheese picnic specially prepared for the two of you. You might even get some help from the waiter at your favorite restaurant. (Just ask him to serve the ring box along with your love's dessert.) Put on your thinking cap and dream a little. Your options are as limitless as your imagination.

Anniversary Celebrations

Whether you are married, living together, or simply ensconced in a long-term relationship, the anniversary is high on the list of commemorative celebrations. Because relationship situations vary from couple to couple, though, the event that's actually being celebrated may vary as well. For some, it may be their wedding day. For others, it may be the day they moved in together. Still others may celebrate the day they met, the day of their first date, or any other number of "firsts." Make no mistake, though: Anniversaries are important. If you think I'm kidding, just miss one. You'll find yourself in a hole so deep that all the sweet talk in the world will never get you out.

The wedding anniversary is a given, so if you're married, commit that date to memory and don't let anything—not work, illness, or death itself—get in the way. If you're not married, though, it's a good idea to talk about which anniversary you're going to celebrate. Keep it to one a year. That way, you can do it up right and make it more than just an event. You can turn it into the sort of unforgettable occasion that memories are made of.

Traditional Etiquette vs. Reality

Although books on etiquette often make our lives easier, they are the pits when it comes to celebrating the anniversary. That's because they all contain a traditional list of anniversary gifts. That may not seem so bad, but the gifts listed aren't going to be well-received by your mate unless you've been together for 10 years or better. Think I'm kidding? Then try this on for size: According to tradition, the first year anniversary should be commemorated with a clock or a gift made of paper. The second year it's cotton, and the third it's glass.

Then it goes from bad to worse. Traditional gifts for other years include such horrors as appliances, wood, iron, wool, linens, and pottery. It doesn't even get good until the 10th year, and even then you may not get the traditional jewelry. Your mate could opt for one of the less expensive traditional items—and that could mean something constructed of tin or aluminum.

The anniversary is supposed to be a celebration of your once-in-a-lifetime, I-can't-live-without-you love for each other. So what's with this junk? If my husband had wrapped up six rolls of paper towels, a package of paper plates, and a box of stationery for our first anniversary, we wouldn't still be together. In fact, the wrapping wouldn't have even made it to the trash before I'd have picked up the phone and called a good attorney. We'd have been in divorce court the next day: end of romance, end of marriage, end of story.

Fortunately for our marriage, my husband isn't much of a traditionalist when it comes to anniversary gifts. He opted, instead, to err on the side of romance. What I unwrapped on our first anniversary didn't involve paper at all. Instead, it was something that tradition didn't allow for until we'd been married for 55 years, something I may not have otherwise lived to see: a diamond and emerald bracelet.

I was stunned. I was delighted, ecstatic, and teary-eyed all at the same time. Despite the fact that my emotions were fluxing and flexing like never before, of one thing I was certain: I knew that my husband loved me absolutely and without question.

Do yourself a favor. *Never* check one of those etiquette books when it comes to anniversary gifts. If your mate wants paper products, he or she will buy them. The same is true of clocks, linens, and other household items. Take a tip from my husband and don't worry about tradition. It's much better to err on the side of romance and give a gift that truly expresses your love. If you don't, you may not have to worry about next year's gift. In fact, you may not have an anniversary to celebrate at all.

Great Gift Ideas

An anniversary gift doesn't have to be expensive to be appropriate. It does have to come from the heart. It does have to fully express the way you feel. And, of course, it does have to make your mate feel much more special than anyone else on the planet. If you already have a great gift in mind, go for it. If you don't, though, don't despair. Just try one of the great tips presented here. They're not only guaranteed to bring the results you want, but to make your mate feel more loved than anyone else in the world.

❧ **Send flowers.** As they are on Valentine's Day, flowers are a standard for the anniversary. Don't just send flowers and call it good, though. That could spell trouble on this day. Use them, instead, as a prologue or teaser to the anniversary gift. They'll put your mate in a wonderfully romantic mood all day long, and that's exactly what this day is all about.

❧ **Make a memory book.** Remember those date souvenirs and mementos we talked about in Chapter 5? Now is the time to use them. Simply organize them into a scrapbook that chronicles your life together. Add photographs, cards you sent each other, bits of old love letters, and brochures from the places you've visited together. When everything's in place, add some captions and romantic messages. Your mate will be more than thrilled; in fact, this gift is sure to become one of his or her most cherished possessions.

❧ **Give a framed all-star mate certificate.** Though I made this for my husband as an add-on gift one year, it turned out to be the gift he treasured the most. He was so proud of it, in fact, that he hung it where everyone could see it. If this idea appeals to you, I suggest working up something on the computer rather than buying a standard, fill-in-the-blank one. That way you can say exactly what you feel. Be sweet. Be sappy. Be romantic. Write down everything your heart would say if it could only speak. Then sign it, date it, frame it, and wrap it. Because it's a gift straight from the heart—your heart—your mate will treasure it always.

ᘓ **Give gifts with a lover's theme.** Although this advice could encompass literally hundreds of gift items, the key here is to be sure that your selection is not only elegant but whispers "romance" rather than "sex." If it doesn't, you're not likely to be enjoying the latter—at least, not on this day! For example, a stained-glass sun-catcher that depicts a hand holding a heart in its palm speaks romance. The same goes for a small replicated statuary of "The Kiss," or a vow of your undying love engraved on a simple piece of jewelry. If none of these appeal to you, simply run an Internet search on "romance." The Web sites that pop up have tons of appropriate gift ideas, and something there will be perfectly suited to your mate and your budget.

The Anniversary Dinner

An elegant dinner is another standard when it comes to celebrating an anniversary. In fact, you can't have a real anniversary celebration without one. Although you can certainly make reservations at a fancy restaurant, such places aren't always conducive to romance. The reasons are many. Even with reservations, you may be in for a lengthy wait. The food may not be up to par or the service may be poor. But the main reason has nothing to do with those. Simply put, restaurants are noisy. There's lots of hustle and bustle. You catch bits and pieces of other conversations, and this makes it difficult to concentrate on your own private exchange. In fact, you may not even hear the sweet nothings that your partner's trying to whisper. And on such a special evening—an evening when nothing should matter but your love for each other—that would indeed be a pity.

For that reason, a sumptuous meal at home is a much better plan. However it's important to do it right. This means getting out the tablecloth and napkins, using your best dishes, and preparing elegant place settings. Although this may not call for something as formal as a centerpiece or place cards, don't forget the candles. Nothing spells romance like a candlelight dinner for two, especially in the privacy of your own home.

I can almost see the furrow in your brow at this point. You're thinking that there's no way you'll feel like romance if you've spent the whole day working on table settings and slaving over a hot stove. You're right, but it doesn't have to be that way. Most dinners can be prepared the day before and warmed up in the microwave just before serving. That way, you'll have plenty of time to put yourself in the mood for romance and thoroughly enjoy the fruits of the evening. It's the perfect solution and well worth the effort.

For your convenience, recipes for my favorite anniversary dinner follow. I'm a meat-eater, but if you and yours are vegetarians, substitute a meatless dish for beef stroganoff. Not sure what's appropriate? Check out *Recipes From A Vegetarian Goddess* by Karri Allrich. The recipes in this book are so delectable, they even make *my* mouth water!

Appetizer: Stuffed Mushroom Caps

6 large mushrooms
1-1/2 oz. shredded cheddar cheese
1 small onion, finely chopped
1 clove minced garlic
1/4 c. dry bread or cracker crumbs
2 T. butter
1 T. dry white wine
1 T. parsley flakes
1-1/2 tsp. lime juice
1/2 tsp. dried oregano
Black pepper to taste

Carefully remove the stems from the mushrooms. Chop finely and set aside. Using a medium skillet, melt the butter and add the mushroom caps. Saute until mushrooms are light brown in color. Remove the caps, drain, and place on an ungreased cookie sheet.

Saute the onion until it's clear. Add the wine. Simmer for a minute or two. Add all remaining ingredients except for the cheese and mix well. Stuff the caps with the mixture and sprinkle with cheese. Place under the broiler for two to three minutes or until the cheese melts. Serve hot.

Entrée: Beef Stroganoff

1 lb. beef round steak, cut into thin strips
2 4-oz. cans mushrooms, drained
1/2 c. sour cream
Broth (3 beef bouillon cubes dissolved in 1-1/2 c. hot water)
3 T. melted butter
2 T. flour
2 T. vegetable oil
2 T. tomato paste
1 gallon-sized plastic zippered bag
Medium-width egg noodles, cooked

Place the beef and flour in the plastic bag, zip shut, and shake until the meat is well coated. Pour the oil and butter into a large skillet and add the beef. Brown well on medium high, then stir in the mushrooms. Gradually add the broth to the skillet, and bring the mixture to a boil. Reduce the heat to low.

Combine sour cream and tomato paste. Add the mixture to the skillet, stirring well. Cook on low for 20–25 minutes. Serve hot over noodles.

Side Dish: Broccoli with Cheese Sauce

1 bag frozen broccoli spears
1/2 c. butter
4 T. flour
1 c. milk
2 c. shredded cheddar cheese
Salt and pepper to taste

Cook the broccoli according to package instructions. Drain and set aside. Melt the butter over low heat in a saucepan. Add the flour and stir well to form a smooth paste. Gradually add the milk one-third cup at a time, making sure to smooth any lumps before adding the next increment. Stirring constantly, simmer on medium heat until the mixture reaches the consistency of cream gravy. Remove from heat and add the cheese, continuing to stir until completely melted. Pour over the broccoli and serve.

Dessert: Chocolate-Mousse Parfaits with Strawberries

1 8-oz. pkg. cream cheese, softened
1-1/2 c. confectioners sugar
1/4 c. granulated sugar
1/3 c. cocoa (unsweetened cocoa, not hot chocolate mix)
1-1/2 c. heavy whipping cream
2 T. milk
5 T. butter, softened
1 tsp. vanilla extract
2–3 milk chocolate candy bars, coarsely grated
1 pint fresh strawberries, halved

Combine the cream cheese and butter, blending until smooth with a spoon or hand mixer. Mix the cocoa with the confectioners sugar, and add it to the butter/cream cheese mixture along with vanilla and milk. Beat until smooth. Fold in the whipping cream and beat until the mixture forms peaks.

Beginning and ending with a spoonful of grated chocolate, layer the mousse and chocolate into parfait glasses. Top with strawberry halves. Chill until ready to serve.

The Anniversary Toast

Because wine denotes a special occasion, it's definitely in order when it comes to the anniversary dinner. (If you prefer nonalcoholic beverages but still want to serve something special, try sparkling cider.) There's more to it than that, though. A special beverage provides a reason to toast your mate, your love, and your relationship. In short, it gives you an excuse to verbalize all those sweet and mushy thoughts that roll around in your head—thoughts you'd never have the nerve to express otherwise.

One-line joke toasts are best saved for another time. Just say something from the heart. It doesn't have to be fancy or poetic. Even a simple "to the only person in the world who takes my breath away" will do. Know that whatever slips from your tongue at this point will set the mood for the rest of the evening. Handle it with romance in mind, and the night will bloom full force.

Need a little help? Just try one of these toasts. They're sure to set the mood for the most romantic evening of your life!

- ଓଷ "My body may grow old, but my heart will never tire of loving you."

- ଓଷ "What joy is there in drinking wine, when I am totally intoxicated with your love?"

- ଓଷ "Many people have caught my eye, but only you could capture my heart."

- ଓଷ "Eternity is much too short to fully express my love for you."

☙ "I love my life because it brought us together; I love you because you are my life."

☙ "You are more than a dream come true. You are my every fantasy."

☙ "My heart shall never beat for anyone but you."

☙ "An anniversary isn't necessary to remind me of my love for you. I celebrate that treasure every day of my life."

Other Delectable Ideas

☙ **Feed each other the appetizer.** There's something inexplicably romantic about feeding each other, especially when it comes to finger foods. Are you worried that the stuffed mushrooms could be a bit messy? Don't be. Your mate will be more than happy to lick away any morsel that might stick to your fingers.

☙ **Play footsies under the table.** This can be great fun while eating the entrée. Start out slowly caressing each other's feet, then work your way up your partner's leg. Let your imagination run wild. You may not even make it to dessert.

☙ **Take your dessert to bed.** Because parents usually frown upon eating anywhere other than the dining room table, few people ever know the delicious, decadent feeling that comes from eating in bed. You're grown now, though, and Mom can't see you. So live a little. Pack up that chocolate mousse and head for the bedroom. Just add a little imagination and see what delights await you.

Winter Holidays

Whether you know them as Yule, Christmas, Kwaanza, Hanukkah, or by some other name, the Winter holidays are another biggie when it comes to gift-giving. Nearly every culture has some version of Santa: a wonderful, omnipotent spirit who bears gifts and knows who's naughty and nice, and we're expected to follow his lead. At least, with the gifts. The Winter holidays are no time to come up empty-handed.

Holiday shopping is perplexing at best, even if you know what to buy for your mate. That's usually not the case, though. Most of us have no idea. We just struggle through the crowds hoping that something—anything—will jump right out at us. Having a mate who is difficult to shop for only compounds the problem. And though you may finally come home with something, you can just forget about keeping any semblance of personal sanity. By the time you're done, you won't have any. It may as well have flown right out the chimney with good ol' St. Nick!

Fortunately, it doesn't have to be this way. The Winter holidays give us more leeway than the birthday, anniversary, or Valentine's Day. This means that it's perfectly fine to mix in items that are necessary with those more personal in nature. Because you'll be giving your love more than one gift, that's good news. The only rule of thumb with holiday gift-giving is that the items in question must be gifts, not presents.

Presents vs. Gifts

Simply put, a present is one of two things. It could be something that you want your mate to have and use. But more than likely, it's something that you secretly want for yourself. You buy it hoping against hope that your mate won't really like it and will toss it aside. You hope that, in the end, you'll wind up with it anyway.

A gift, on the other hand, is much, much more. It's something selected expressly with your mate in mind, something that he or she would enjoy, and something specifically suited to personal style and taste. Although a gift can be useful, necessary, or even just a little bit frivolous, it often doesn't serve any mundane purpose at all. Its only real function is to make your mate happy.

It's perfectly permissible to give a holiday gift that's functional and necessary, but there are a few items you'll want to stay away from when buying for Princess Perfect, unless, of course, she specifically requests them. These fall under the categories of household appliances and kitchen appliances and accoutrements. Make this mistake once, and she'll never forget it. (She'll never let you forget it, either.)

Many years ago, for example, I excitedly sat by the tree waiting to unwrap the one little package with my name on it. I'd been told it held something really special, and I'd been waiting for weeks to rip it open. The anticipation was tremendous, and I could hardly wait to see what was inside.

Of course, I'd imagined all sorts of wonderful items: a bottle of my favorite perfume, something personalized with my name on it, or maybe even a fabulous piece of jewelry packaged with a few rocks to throw me off on the weight and size. When I finally tore through the paper, though, what I found was anything but wonderful. In fact, I'd have been happier with a sack full of coal. The object of all my anticipation was nothing more than an electric can opener.

At first, I thought it was a joke, but one look at my ex's pleased face told me it wasn't. Even worse, he thought he'd done something marvelous and wonderful. Once the damnable thing shot through the air accompanied by a lengthy stream of expletives, though, he knew better. It was a mistake he never repeated and an episode that (even some 20-odd years later) I never forgot.

Minimizing Shopping Woes

As with the birthday, it's a good idea to discuss what you would like to have in the way of holiday gifts. You may want to limit your discussion to one large item for each of you, though. Why? Because this particular season epitomizes the magic of childlike wonder, you will want to leave room for the element of surprise. Leave it out, and the holidays lose all appeal. In fact, they won't be any fun at all.

This leaves an opening for all sorts of smaller gifts. Shopping for your mate can be fun, but it can also be very time-consuming. With that in mind, shop early. You'll not only avoid the hustle and bustle of holiday crowds, but you'll save time and money. More important, though, you'll save your nerves. The last thing you need is a heavy dose of stress during the holiday season.

If you really want to relieve the pressures of holiday shopping, handle it through the ease of mail order. Thumb through magazines and catalogs. Even better, surf the Internet. The latter puts virtually anything (even hard-to-find items) right at your fingertips. Best of all, you'll be able to shop at your leisure from home, and there's nothing more relaxing than that!

Great Gift Ideas

Even though you already know to steer clear of household and kitchen appliances, there are some gifts that bring more pleasure than others. That being the case, a few ideas are listed here. They're not only guaranteed to bring lots of smiles but also many wonderful holiday memories in the years to come.

- ⊂ℬ **The holiday stocking.** My husband filled one of these for me last year, and it was one of the most remarkable gifts I received. Most of the goodies inside weren't expensive. Most of them I could have purchased myself. What made it so special, though, was that he'd gone to the trouble to select each item specifically with me in mind. Give one of these to your mate, and the smiles will just keep coming!

- ⊂ℬ **Personalized items.** People just love things that tout their names, so personalized items (coffee cups, key rings, notepads, pen and pencil sets, and so on) make wonderful holiday gifts. If you're looking for something really different, check novelty catalogs and order in some personalized playing cards. It's a gift your mate will never forget.

- ⊂ℬ **Perfume or aftershave.** Though this can be expensive (especially if your mate's tastes lean toward designer fragrances) you can't go wrong here as long as you buy your mate's favorite. You'll get extra points if you get it right the first time!

- ⊂ℬ **Hobby-related gifts.** This can include anything from sporting goods to camera equipment, art supplies to quilting fabrics. It's just a matter of where your mate's interests lie. Any gift that relates to a hobby is not only a safe bet but one that will get plenty of use through the coming year.

ᐊ **Business-oriented gifts.** If your mate's been need-
ing a new briefcase, desk set, or other business-
related accoutrement, now is the time to give it.
Have it monogrammed or engraved with his or her
name or initials to add a really special touch.

Miscellaneous and Sundry

We've covered the major gift-giving holidays, but there
are a few other occasions to keep in mind if you plan on
living happily ever after. Some involve you directly and others
don't. Make no mistake, though: It's up to you to see that
they're celebrated properly and given their due.

ᐊ **New Year's Eve.** Gifts really aren't necessary, but
this is one evening that the two of you should
spend together. It doesn't matter whether you stay
up to see the New Year in or not. It's only important that it be a special evening along with some
good old-fashioned reminiscing and maybe a glass
or two of champagne!

ᐊ **Mother's Day and Father's Day.** If you have children at home, it's up to you to see that they remember the honoree with a nice gift. Take
younger kids shopping and remind the older ones
so they aren't empty-handed when the big day
arrives. If your kids are grown and gone, you're
still not off the hook. In this case, though, a nice
lunch at your mate's favorite restaurant will do
the trick.

☙ **Miscellaneous turning points.** Just as life deals out trials and tribulations, it also rewards us with turning points worthy of celebration. These might include a job promotion, a raise, or some other fabulous stroke of good luck. When these arise, be quick to acknowledge them. You don't have to make a big fuss. It's only important that you honor your mate in some way. A special dinner, a bouquet of flowers, or a token gift is appropriate.

One More Thing

If you really want to live happily ever after, you'll undoubtedly have to keep the happiness growing. It's going to need a boost now and then, something more than a kiss or a present. In fact, it's going to have to be something way beyond anything that any form of humankind or mundanity can offer. That something, of course, is a little magic.

The best way to accomplish this is to perform one of the spells outlined here. Don't worry that the laws of karma will get you for manipulation. Anything that brings joy and happiness to everyone concerned can't be bad. I only wish that someone had once thought to "manipulate" me in such a fashion. I'd have been on my way to happily ever after years ago!

Silver Maple Spell

(Note: Only perform this spell if you own your property or have permission to plant trees on the property you lease.)

Materials list:

    2 silver maple saplings (no substitutions)
    12 fertilizer sticks

On a Friday during the new to waxing moon, dig a hole large enough to accommodate the saplings on each side of your front yard. Plant the trees and water them thoroughly. Then gather six of the fertilizer sticks and kneel by one of the trees. Shove one of the sticks into the ground near the base and say:

    By stick of one, disharmony's done

Moving in a clockwise fashion, push a second stick into the ground and say:

    By stick of two, we lose all rue

With the third say:

    By stick of three, our joy flows free

With the fourth say:

    By stick of four, love opens the door

With the fifth say:

    By stick of five, delight is alive

With the sixth say:

    By stick of six, our happiness fix

Repeat this process with the second tree. Then stand between the two saplings and say:

All who live within this place—
Its structure, boundaries, or outdoor
    space
Shall always find happiness in their
    hearts
And from their cores, it may not part
By Lord and Lady numbered Three
As I will, so mote it be

Tend the trees thereafter, taking care to water and fertilize them as necessary.

Long-Term Happiness Spell

Materials list:

1 pink candle
1 red permanent marker
6 whole cloves
Pencil
Matches or a cigarette lighter

Begin by completely coloring the outside of the pink candle with the red marker. (Don't forget to cover the candle top and bottom.) As you color, chant:

With red for lust and pink for love
I conjure joy now from above

Then using the pencil, draw a small heart (about an inch in size) on the candle. Push the cloves firmly into the candle (you may need to soften the wax with a match or the lighter to do this effectively) using one clove each at the curved tops of the heart. Then insert one clove at the bottom point of the heart, one clove at the inverted point between the curves, and one clove on each side of the heart to frame its shape. As you attach the cloves, say:

> I frame our life with love and spice
> So happiness is now enticed
> To come and stay and live within
> Our hearts as magic starts to spin

Light the candle and visualize the two of you experiencing true joy. If something else creeps in (stress, depression, or whatever) quickly replace it with happiness. Hold the picture for a minute or two, then say:

> Heart to heart and hand to hand
> Perfect joy I now demand
> Bring us happiness untold
> As this flame burns bright and bold
> Continue on once it's burned out
> So laughter from our lips rings out

Let the candle burn down, and collect the cloves and any leftover wax. Place them under the bed to work while you sleep. Flush them down the toilet when you replace them the following month.

The Last Word

By the time you get to this section, you should have all the information you need to live happily ever after. It's all in this book and you can refer to it at any time. The real key to keeping that breathless, I-can't-live-without-you feeling alive and well, though, is something that we all instinctively know but tend to forget from time to time.

Simply put–

Making love is not an act. It has no beginning. It has no end. It's not some enjoyable project that you start and do and finish. It is something, instead, that you do every moment of every single day that you're together, whether you're sweeping the floor, taking out the trash, or simply watching TV. Both intangible and concrete, it lives in your core, sings in your heart, and radiates from your smile. That's what making love is all about. The sooner you put it into practice, the sooner you'll have what you always dreamed of: that once-in-a-lifetime romance that you thought was possible only in the fairy tales.

Appendix A

Magical Associations of Herbs, Plants, and Flowers

Beauty

Avocado
Catnip
Flax
Ginseng
Maidenhair fern
Rose
Rosemary
Witch hazel

Courage

Borage
Cedar
Columbine
Musterwort
Mullein
Sweet pea
Thyme
Tonka bean
Vanilla
Yarrow

Heartbreak Management

Apple
Bittersweet
Cyclamen
Honeysuckle
Jasmine
Lemon balm
Magnolia
Peach

Strawberry
Yarrow

Joy

Catnip
Celandine
Daisy
Hawthorn
Honeysuckle
Hyacinth
Lemon balm
Lily of the valley
Marjoram
Morning glory
Saffron
Shepherd's purse

Love

Adam and Eve root
Allspice
Apple
Apricot
Balm of Gilead
Basil
Bleeding heart
Cardamom
Catnip
Chamomile
Cinnamon
Clove
Columbine
Copal

Coriander
Crocus
Cubeb
Daffodil
Daisy
Damiana
Dill
Elecampane
Elm
Endive
Fig
Gardenia
Geranium
Ginger
Ginseng
Hibiscus
Hyacinth
Indian paintbrush
Jasmine
Juniper
Kava kava
Lady's mantle
Lavender
Lemon balm
Lemon verbena
Linden
Lobelia
Lotus
Loveage
Maidenhair fern
Mandrake
Maple
Marjoram

Myrtle
Nutmeg
Orchid
Pansy
Peach
Peppermint
Periwinkle
Poppy
Primrose
Rose
Rosemary
Rue
Saffron
Skullcap
Spearmint
Spiderwort
Strawberry
Thyme
Tonka bean
Tulip
Vanilla
Vervain
Violet
Willow
Wood betony
Yarrow

Lust

Allspice
Caraway
Carrot
Cattail

Cinnamon
Cinquefoil
Clove
Damiana
Deerstongue
Dill
Foxglove
Galangal
Ginseng
Hibiscus
Mistletoe
Parsley
Rosemary
Sesame
Southernwood
Vanilla
Violet
Yohimbe

Comfrey
Hops
Lavender
Nettle
Oats
St. John's wort
Passonflower
Skullcap

Success

Cinnamon
Clover
Ginger
High John
Lemon balm
Orange
Rowan

Stress Management

Calendula
Chamomile

Victory

Bay leaf
High John
Olive

Appendix B

Magical Associations
of Stones

Beauty

Amber
Cat's eye
Jasper
Opal
Rose quartz
Unakite

Courage

Agate
Amethyst
Aquamarine
Bloodstone
Carnelian
Diamond
Hematite
Lapis lazuli
Tigereye
Watermelon tourmaline
Turquoise

Eloquence

Carnelian
Celestite
Emerald
Turquoise

Joy

Orange calcite
Chrysoprase
Sunstone
Unakite

Love

Alexandrite
Amber
Amethyst
Chrysocolla
Diamond
Emerald
Jade
Lapis lazuli
Lepidolite
Malachite
Moonstone
Opal
Pearl
Rose quartz
Rhodocrosite
Sapphire
Topaz
Pink tourmaline
Turquoise

Lust

- Carnelian
- Coral
- Mahogany obsidian
- Sunstone

Stress Management

- Amethyst
- Jade
- Brecciated jasper
- Paua shell

Peaceful Separation

- Black onyx
- Black tourmaline

Success

- Amazonite
- Chrysoprase
- Marble

Appendix C

Magical Associations of Deities

For further information on Deity origin or history, please check the Internet or your public library. Gender is abbreviated below for your convenience.

Beauty

Aphrodite (F)
Apollo (M)
Venus (F)

Courage

Achilles (M)
Apollo (M)
Ares (M)
Artemis (F)
Athena (F)
Atlas (M)
Bellora (F)
Diana (F)
Hercules (M)
Mars (M)
Morgan (F)
Neith (F)
Persephone (F)
Perseus (M)

Eloquence

Sarasvati (F)
The Muses (F)

Heartbreak Management

Apollo (M)
Diana (F)
Gaia (F)
Luna (F)
Selene (F)

Home

Bannik (M)
Cardea (F)
Da-bog (M)
Dugnai (F)
Gucumatz (M)
Hastehogan (M)
Hestia (F)
Kikimora (F)
Neith (F)
The Lares (M)
Penates (M)
Vesta (F)

Joy

Amaterasu (F)
Ataksak (M)

Baldur (M)
Fu-Hsing (M)
Hathor (F)
Hotei (M)
Omacatl (M)
Samkhat (F)
Tien Kuan (M)

Love

Amun Ra (M)
Anat (F)
Angus (M)
Aphrodite (F)
Astarte (F)
Belili (F)
Belit-Ilanit (F)
Benten (F)
Cupid (M)
Cybele (F)
Erzulie (F)
Hathor (F)
Ishtar (F)
Isis (F)
Kama (M)
Venus (F)

Lust

Aphrodite (F)
Arami (F)
Bes (M)
Eros (M)
Hathor (F)
Heket (F)
Indrani (F)
Ishtar (F)
Lalita (F)
Lilith (F)
Min (M)
Pan (M)
Rati (F)
Venus (F)
Yarilo (M)

Success

Anu (F)
Apollo (M)
Diana (F)
Fortuna (F)

Appendix D

*Mail Order
Supply Stores*

Herbs and Arts
215 E. Colfax Avenue
Denver, CO 80206
(303) 388-2544
www.herbsandarts.com

Lady Sprite's Cupboard
3184 E. Indian School Road
Phoenix, AZ 85016
(602) 956-3539
www.ladyspritescupboard.com

Pathways
8980 Watson Road
St. Louis, MO 63119
(314) 842-0047
www.pathwaysstl.com

Points of Light
4358 Stearns Street
Long Beach, CA 90815
(562) 985-3388
www.pointsoflight.com

Raven's Flight
5042 Vineland Avenue
North Hollywood, CA 91601
(888) 84-RAVEN
www.ravensflight.com

Salem West
1209 North High St.
Columbus, OH 43201
(614) 421-7557
www.salemwest.com
www.neopagan.com

Soul Journey
9 Main St.
Butler, NJ 07405
(973) 838-6564
www.souljourney.com

Triple Moon, Inc.
15 Powder Mill Circle
Needham, MA 02942
(781) 453-0363
www.triplemoon.com

Appendix E

Other Ways to Say I Love You

If you can't quite force yourself to say those three little words (even though you mean them), try saying them in another language. Don't worry if you have to translate. After you've mastered the foreign versions, translation will be a snap!

Afrikaans	Ek is lief vir jou
Albanian	Te dua
Amharic	Afekrishalehou
Arabic	Ana Behibek
Armenian	Yes kez si'rumem
Basque	Maite zaitut
Bengali	Ami tomake bahlobashi
Bosnian	Volim te
Bulgarian	Obicham te
Cambodian	Bon sro lanh oon
Cheyenne	Nemehotatse
Chinese	Wo ai ni
Creole	Mi aime jou
Croatian	Volim te
Czech	Miluji tev
Danish	Jeg elsker dig
Dutch	Ik hou van je
Eskimo	Nagligivaget
Esperanto	Mi amas vin
Estonian	Mina armastan sind
Farsi	Asheghetam
Filipino	Mahal Kita
French	Je t'aime
Frisian	Ik hald fan dei
Galician	Querote
German	Ich liebe dich
Greek	S'agapo
Hawaiian	Aloha I'a Au Oe

Hebrew	Ani ohev otach
Hindi	My tumko pyar karta hu
Hungarian	Szeretlek
Icelandic	Eg elska thig
Indonesian	Saya cinta padamu
Irish	T'a gr'a agam dhuit
Italian	Ti amo
Japanese	Kimi a ai shiteru
Klingon	Qabang
Korean	Tangshin-i cho-a-yo
Latvian	Es tevi milu
Lithuanian	As tave myliu
Malaysian	Saya cintamu
Mandarin	Wo ai ni
Mohawk	Konoronhkwa
Norwegian	Jeg elsker deg
Polish	Kocham Cie
Portuguese	Eu te amo
Romanian	Te iubesc
Russian	Ya vas lyublyu
Sanskritt	Wayi snihyaami
Serbian	Volim te
Slovak	Lubim ta
Slovenian	Ljubim te
Spanish	Te amo
Swahili	Nakupenda
Swedish	Jag älskar dig
Tahitian	Ua here vau la oe
Turkish	Seni seviyorum
Ukrainian	Ya tebe kokhayu
Welsh	Rwy'n dy garu di
Yiddish	Kh'hob dikh lib
Zulu	Ngiyakuthanda

Suggested Reading List

Although the magical system in this book was devised from the trial-and-error process of my own personal experiences, there are many other books on the market that give excellent advice for dealing with matters of the heart. For your convenience, some of my favorites are listed here.

Cabot, Tracy. *How to Make a Man Fall in Love With You.* New York: St. Martin's Press, 1984.

Fagan, Nancy. *The Complete Idiot's Guide to Romance.* Indianapolis, Ind.: Macmillan Publishing, 2000.

Hardie, Titania. *Love: Titania's Wishing Spells.* New York: William Morrow & Company, 1999.

Kingma, Daphne Rose. *Weddings from the Heart.* Berkeley, Calif.: Conari Press, 1991.

Knight, Sirona. *Love, Sex, and Magick.* Secaucus, N.J.: Citadel Press, 1999.

MacGregor, Trish. *The Everything Love Spells Mini-book.* Holbrook, Mass.: Adams Media Corporation, 2000.

O'Neal, Janet. *The Complete Idiot's Guide to the Art of Seduction.* New York: Macmillan Publishing, 1999.

Penney, Alexandra. *How to Make Love to a Man.* New York: Clarkson N. Potter, Inc., 1981.

Sarris, Arian. *21 Ways to Attract Your Soulmate.* St. Paul, Minn.: Llewellyn Publications, 2000.

Sophia. *The Little Book of Love Spells.* Kansas City, Mo.: Andrews McMeel Publishing, 1997.

Telesco, Patricia. *A Little Book of Love Magic.* Freedom, Calif.: Crossing Press, 1999.

Index

About the Author

Dorothy Morrison is an award-winning author and an avid practitioner of the Ancient Arts for more than 25 years. She is the author of many successful books of Wiccan interest, including *Everyday Magic*.

Dorothy and her husband live near Washington, D.C., with their black lab.